English

The 13+ Study Book

For the Common Entrance 13+ exams

Practise • Prepare • Pass

Everything your child needs for 13+ success

CONTENTS

Section Six — Types of Writing

Section Seven — Using Language Effectively

Section Eight — The CASE Paper

Section Nine — Grammar

Section Ten — Punctuation

Section Eleven — Spelling

Published by CGP

Editors:
Rachel Grocott, Anna Hall, Holly Poynton, Matt Topping

With thanks to Susan Carrdus and Sabrina Robinson for the proofreading.

With thanks to Laura Jakubowski for the copyright research.

ISBN: 978 1 78294 178 1
Printed by Elanders Ltd, Newcastle upon Tyne.
Clipart from Corel®

Based on the classic CGP style created by Richard Parsons.

13+ English

Well, an introduction seems like a good place to start, so let's get cracking...

There are two **13+ English** exams

1) Whether you're doing Level 1 or Level 2, there are <u>two</u> Common Entrance 13+ English papers.

2) Each exam lasts <u>1 hour 15 minutes</u>, which includes your <u>reading</u> and <u>planning time</u>.

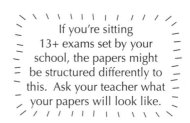

If you're sitting 13+ exams set by your school, the papers might be structured differently to this. Ask your teacher what your papers will look like.

3) Each exam has two sections — one <u>reading section</u> and one <u>writing section</u>, as shown in this <u>handy diagram</u>:

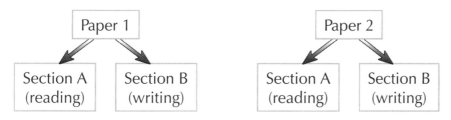

Paper 1 → Section A (reading) / Section B (writing)

Paper 2 → Section A (reading) / Section B (writing)

4) If you're doing the <u>Common Academic Scholarship Examination</u>, there's a <u>different</u> paper — see <u>Section Eight</u> (p.55-58) for more info.

All the exams test your **Reading** and **Writing**

1) Whichever level you're doing, in the <u>reading</u> sections you'll have a piece of <u>prose</u> or a <u>poem</u> (it might be an <u>extract</u> from a poem).

2) You'll then have to read the text <u>carefully</u> and <u>answer</u> some <u>questions</u>. See <u>p.2</u> for more information.

3) The <u>writing</u> sections ask you to write a text from a choice of topics and styles. See <u>p.28</u> for the <u>types</u> of text you might have to write.

Spelling, **Punctuation** and **Grammar** are **Important**

1) The examiner will be looking at your spelling, punctuation, grammar and vocabulary in <u>both sections</u> of the exams.

2) In the exams you need to find a balance between working <u>quickly</u> and working <u>carefully</u>. You don't have much time, but you need to <u>impress</u> the examiner.

3) Luckily for you, this book has lots of handy information about <u>spelling</u> tricky words, <u>punctuating</u> sentences properly, using <u>grammar</u> correctly and how to use dazzling <u>vocabulary</u>.

Testing, testing, one two, one two...

This book is up and running and hopefully you're hearing me loud and clear. There's lots more coming up on both the reading sections and the writing sections, and how to be brilliant at both.

The Reading Section

Whether you're doing Level 1 or Level 2 for 13+ English, you'll sit two exams.

Both exams have a Reading Section

For 13+ English, there are <u>two exams</u>. Each exam has a Section A and a Section B. <u>Section A</u> for both exams is the <u>reading</u> part. Section B is the writing part — see p.28 for more info.

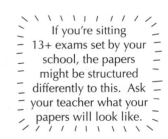
If you're sitting 13+ exams set by your school, the papers might be structured differently to this. Ask your teacher what your papers will look like.

In Paper 1, Section A, there's a passage of <u>prose</u> for you to read. The extract might be from a <u>novel</u>, a <u>play</u>, a <u>biography</u> or a piece of <u>travel writing</u>. You'll then have to answer some <u>questions</u> about it.

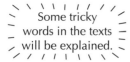
Some tricky words in the texts will be explained.

Paper 2, Section A will contain a piece of <u>poetry</u>. You might get a <u>whole poem</u> or an <u>extract</u> from a longer poem. Then there'll be some <u>questions</u> to answer.

If you're sitting the <u>Common Academic Scholarship Examination</u>, there's a <u>different paper</u> — see <u>Section Eight</u> (p.55-58) for more <u>details</u> about the <u>CASE paper</u>.

Spend 35 Minutes on the Reading Section

1) Each paper lasts <u>1 hour 15 minutes</u>.

2) Each paper is worth <u>50 marks</u> — <u>25 marks</u> for the <u>reading</u> section and <u>25 marks</u> for the <u>writing</u> section.

3) That means you'll have roughly <u>35 minutes</u> for <u>each</u> section, with 5 minutes left at the end to <u>check your work</u> for mistakes.

4) Work <u>quickly</u> but <u>carefully</u> — and always make sure you do <u>what the question asks you</u>.

Look at how many Marks you get for a Question

It's important to look at <u>how many</u> marks you get for <u>each question</u> so you know <u>how long</u> to spend answering each one.

Q What event is Harriet talking about in the first paragraph? [1]

This is only worth <u>one mark</u>, so <u>don't</u> spend ages writing a complicated answer.

Q How does the author build tension in the third paragraph? Support your answer with evidence from the text. [6]

This is worth <u>six marks</u>, so you'll need to give a bit more detail (see p.10-11).

Reading... I thought that was a place in Berkshire?

You're going to have to do a couple of reading exercises in your exams, so it's a good idea to familiarise yourself with the reading section so you know exactly what you'll have to do.

Novels

You might get an extract from a novel in the exam, so you need to know this stuff.

The **Perspective** is **Who** tells the story

Stories are normally written in the <u>first</u> or <u>third</u> person. A story that uses "<u>I</u>" or "<u>we</u>" is written in the <u>first</u> person. A story that uses "<u>he</u>", "<u>she</u>" or "<u>they</u>" is written in the <u>third</u> person.

| I decided to join the circus. | She decided to join the circus. |

This is in the <u>first person</u>. It makes the text seem more <u>personal</u> and <u>immediate</u>.

This is in the <u>third person</u>. It makes the text feel <u>less personal</u>.

The **Plot** is **What Happens**

The <u>plot</u> of a story is all the things that happen, in the <u>right order</u>.
A plot needs a <u>beginning</u>, a <u>middle</u> and an <u>end</u>.

Beginning	**Middle**	**End**
Jimmy has lost his dog.	Jimmy asks the neighbours if they've seen his dog. They haven't.	Jimmy finds the dog — it was sleeping under a pile of clothes.

The **Setting** is **Where** it **Happens**

Writers choose their settings <u>carefully</u>.
Where the story takes place is <u>important</u> for creating an <u>atmosphere</u>.

A science fiction story could be set in outer space.

A horror story could be set in an old haunted house.

The **Theme** is the **Deeper Meaning**

Themes include <u>love</u>, <u>greed</u>, <u>family</u>, <u>power</u> etc.

Example

The theme of most fairy tales is good against evil. The good characters always win in the end. For example, Cinderella went to the ball and married the prince, and her ugly sisters got nothing.

Remember, remember the fifth of November...

The terms on this page are nice and simple — make sure you know them. Most stories have a perspective, plot, setting and theme. Learn the page well so you know what to look out for.

Plays

Reading plays can get pretty confusing. But fear not! This page should make things simpler.

Plays are written to be *Acted*

1) There is a <u>massive difference</u> between a play and a novel or short story. A novel tells a story by <u>describing</u> it to you. A play tells a story by <u>showing</u> it to you.

2) You <u>don't</u> usually get any long describing bits in a play. The actors show the audience what's going on by the <u>way</u> they say their lines, as well as <u>what</u> they say.

3) The audience <u>doesn't</u> have the <u>play script</u> in front of them, so the <u>actors</u> have to do all the <u>work</u>.

When you read a play, you often have to work out what's going on just by reading the text and stage directions.

Stage Directions give a few clues

1) Stage directions show actors <u>what to do</u>, when to <u>come in</u> and when to <u>leave</u> the stage.

2) They're the words in <u>brackets</u>, and they tell you the basics of what's <u>happening</u>.

3) <u>Always</u> read them when you read a play.

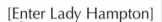

[Enter Lady Hampton]

"<u>Enter</u>" is a <u>stage direction</u>. It tells the person playing Lady Hampton to walk on stage.

[Exeunt Lord Hampton and Archie]

"<u>Exeunt</u>" is a daft word. All it means is that <u>more than one</u> person leaves the stage.

The *Director* decides the rest

1) Sometimes the stage directions <u>tell</u> the actors how to say their lines.

CHRIS [angrily] I cannot believe you broke another window!

"<u>Angrily</u>" is a <u>stage direction</u>. It tells the actor playing Chris <u>how</u> to say this line.

2) More often, though, the <u>director</u> has to work out how the actors should say the lines — sadly, joyfully or whatever.

3) Unfortunately, you don't have a director in the test — you've got to figure it <u>all</u> out for yourself, from the <u>words</u>.

It might help if you try to imagine that you're the director. Ask yourself how you would direct the actors in the play you're reading.

Plays for insects — written to bee acted...

It seems pretty weird to me. They're all written to be acted on stage, but you have to read them. Try and imagine what's happening on stage as you read... and don't forget the stage directions.

Travel Writing

Travel writing is like a diary written for someone else — it's really personal and very detailed.

Travel writing is full of Detailed Description

1) Travel writers work really hard to <u>build up an image</u> of the <u>people</u> and <u>places</u> they have seen.

2) There's always loads of <u>detail</u> and a big focus on <u>setting</u>.

> I looked at the road stretching before me like a shiny black ribbon. The air was intolerably close and a bead of sweat dropped from my forehead as I surveyed the dark, moody horizon.

Look out for <u>descriptive</u> and <u>imaginative</u> language.
Think about how the writer is using his or her <u>senses</u>.

It's usually written in the First Person

1) Travel writing is often written from a <u>first-person perspective</u>, so the author will use 'I' a lot.

2) The writer is recording their own <u>personal</u> reaction to their surroundings, so they often talk about their <u>thoughts</u> and <u>feelings</u>.

3) The writer is trying to make you <u>feel like you are there</u> with them. But remember — everything is from <u>their perspective</u> — it's a bit like you're seeing it <u>through their eyes</u>.

> Travel writers aren't shy — they're usually very quick to let you know how they <u>feel</u> about the people and places they are describing.

Travel writing can have Several Purposes

1) The main point of travel writing is to be <u>entertaining</u>. The writer wants to grab your attention with the <u>exciting</u> or <u>amazing</u> things they are <u>describing</u>.

2) They also want to give you <u>information</u> about the places they've been to.

3) So the purpose of the text is to <u>entertain</u> and <u>inform</u>.

<u>Descriptive</u> language <u>informs</u> the reader.

<u>Humour</u> is used to <u>entertain</u> the reader.

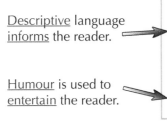

> As the train chugged steadily through the beautiful, sloping valleys, I sat back and thought about how lucky I'd been. I took a deep breath and glanced up at the vibrant and charming woman I had just met. Then, to my horror, a monkey jumped out of her hat...

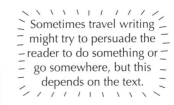

Sometimes travel writing might try to persuade the reader to do something or go somewhere, but this depends on the text.

Let me entertain you...

Or I could just tell you about this great holiday I went on? Travel writing is entertaining and informative — keep this in mind while you're answering the questions and you won't go far wrong.

Biographies and Autobiographies

Now for some more personal stuff. This time it's all about biographies and autobiographies...

Biographies and *Autobiographies* are *Different*

1) A biography is an account of someone's life story written by someone else.

2) An autobiography is an account of someone's life story written by that person.

3) Both biographies and autobiographies focus on the important moments in that person's life.

> At twenty-five, Ian became a father for the first time. → This is from a biography.

> The day I got married was the happiest day of my life. → This is from an autobiography.

Biographies are written in the *Third Person*

1) Biographies are written in the third person.

2) They're usually in the past tense as they're an account of events that have already happened.

3) Biographies usually only take into account the author's version of the events, so they're often biased (or one-sided).

Third person pronouns are used.

This is all written in the past tense.

> Stuart was elected as town mayor in July 1854. He was the best mayor that Newtron ever had and led the town's rugby team to a glorious victory over Protown in 1857. Stuart was replaced as mayor in 1862 after a controversial election.

Watch out for language that is subjective or biased.

Autobiographies are a bit like *Diaries*

1) Autobiographies are written in the first person and are extremely personal. They give lots of detail about the important moments in a person's life, and how the person felt about them.

2) The writer normally writes about events in a chronological order, and explains how these experiences have moulded his or her personality.

3) They are often very touching, but they are written with the audience in mind — the writer is aiming to entertain and persuade the reader.

> January was a really tough month that year. Losing my job was a big blow, especially with all that Christmas debt that needed shifting. I was at an all-time low and began to make some really bad decisions...

This account is moving — you feel sympathy for the writer's situation.

The writer is trying to persuade you to look at things their way. They want to justify their choices and get you to believe their side of the story.

Don't just take my word for it...

...but if it's an autobiography, that's all you can do. Biographies and autobiographies tell you lots about someone, but remember — they're completely one-sided, so take them with a pinch of salt.

Section Two — Reading: The Basics

Poems

Petrified of poetry? Don't worry — this page will help you to start tackling poetry questions.

There are **Different Types** of **Poem**

Not all poems are the same. These are some different kinds of poem you might run into:

BALLADS are poems that tell a story. They often have four-line verses and a chorus.

FREE VERSE is a type of poem which doesn't rhyme and doesn't have a set line length.

SONNETS are usually 14 lines long, and have a special rhyme pattern.

A **Verse** is a **Section** of a poem

1) Poems are made up of lines.
2) Lines in a poem are often repeated.
3) A group of lines in a poem is called a verse — a verse is also known as a stanza.
4) Verses in a poem usually have different words, but they often follow the same rhyme pattern.

A **Poem** fits **A Lot** into a **Small Space**

In a poem, how things are said is just as important as what is said.
Here's a couple of verses from the poem 'The Brook' by Alfred Lord Tennyson.

Think about why particular words have been chosen — each word needs to say a lot. E.g. Why has Tennyson chosen "eddying" here rather than "gushing" or "churning"?

I chatter over stony ways,
In little sharps and trebles,
I bubble into eddying bays,
I babble on the pebbles.

I slip, I slide, I gloom, I glance,
Among my skimming swallows;
I make the netted sunbeam dance
Against my sandy shallows.

Figurative language e.g. imagery — is used to make the poem more interesting.

There's more on figurative language on p.14-15.

Rhyme and rhythm affect how the poem sounds. They put the focus on particular words. See p.19-20 for more info.

Learn this page on poetry — it could be verse...

It's hard to write a poem about poetry. Almost nothing rhymes with "poem". Weird, eh?
Just make sure you know about the different types of poem and what verses (or stanzas) are.

Tackling Reading Questions

Now you know the types of text you might get asked about, it's time to deal with the questions...

Skim-Read the bit of writing First

1) When you're dealing with the <u>reading section</u> of your exam paper, you should <u>read</u> the bit of writing first, and then <u>read the questions</u>.

2) When you read the bit of writing, you should <u>skim-read</u>. Skim-reading gives a <u>rough idea</u> of what the bit of writing is about. It's like looking at something <u>quickly</u> and having a <u>blurred</u> picture of it in your head. Look at it <u>carefully</u>, and you get more detail.

It's a bit like this.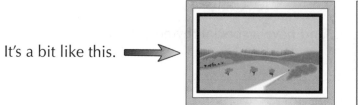

3) You can <u>jot down</u> any <u>key points</u> (like names or important events — see p.9), but don't spend long doing it.

Work Out what the questions are Asking

1) The questions will be about <u>the stuff you've just read</u>. You must read through each question very <u>carefully</u> before you even think about answering it.

2) Always remember the <u>magic question</u>:

What is the question asking me to do?

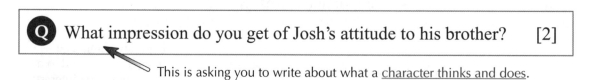

Q What impression do you get of Josh's attitude to his brother? [2]

This is asking you to write about what a <u>character thinks and does</u>.

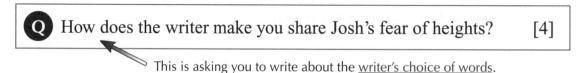

Q How does the writer make you share Josh's fear of heights? [4]

This is asking you to write about the <u>writer's choice of words</u>.

3) Whatever else you do, make sure your <u>answer</u> matches what the <u>question</u> is asking you to do. It's amazing how <u>easy</u> it is to slip up this way.

4) There's <u>no point</u> spending all your time in the first question talking about the writer's choice of words. Even if you do it <u>brilliantly</u>, it still won't be the right answer.

Questions — always looking for answers...

Skim-reading can save you time and help you get to grips with the text quickly. Hurray. Don't then go and waste all that good work by not answering the question you've been asked. Boo.

Section Two — Reading: The Basics

Finding the Important Bits

You have to agree — it's much easier to remember key points than a load of words.

Scan the writing for Key Words and Phrases

1) Once you've worked out <u>what</u> the question is <u>asking you</u>, you'll need to <u>go back to the text</u> and look for <u>key words</u> and <u>phrases</u>.

2) The <u>key words</u> and <u>key phrases</u> in a sentence or a paragraph give you the real <u>nitty-gritty</u> of what it means. They're the things you'll need to <u>answer the questions</u>.

3) When you want to <u>find</u> those key bits of information, it's much <u>quicker</u> to let your eyes wander over the page on the <u>lookout</u> for the words you want. This is called <u>scanning</u>.

Find the bits that Answer the Question

Q In what ways does the article make readers want to visit the castle?   [4]

1) The key to answering questions like this is to <u>find loads of things in the article</u> that help answer the question. This is where you need to scan for <u>key words</u> and <u>phrases</u>.

2) Here's the start of the article with the bits you <u>need</u> and the bits you <u>don't need</u> helpfully pointed out...

You <u>don't</u> need to say <u>where</u> the castle is.

Mention that it <u>looks</u> <u>mysterious</u> — that makes it sound interesting.

People would want to visit to find out more about the <u>stories</u> and <u>secrets</u>.

You <u>don't</u> need to <u>retell</u> these stories in your answer. Just say that the writer mentions them.

The <u>writer spends some time talking about the dungeon</u>. People find horrible things fascinating, so this bit is <u>important</u>.

> Callendale Castle is built on a hill overlooking the village of Callendale in West Bassetshire. On approaching Callendale village, the twin towers of the castle suddenly loomed through the mist, giving the village a mysterious appearance.
>
> Callendale Castle holds many stories, and many secrets. A quick read through the guidebook gave me a colourful insight into the way things must have been inside these forbidding stone walls all those years ago. A secret meeting between King Henry V and a French ambassador took place here during the Hundred Years War. In 1814, the castle narrowly escaped being burnt to the ground when a lazy kitchen boy left a pig roasting on the open fire unattended.
>
> The castle tour took me to a dark, dank dungeon, complete with gruesome instruments of torture. Hidden in one corner is a tiny cell, little more than a hole, where countless prisoners were left to rot away.

3) There'll always be loads of stuff that's got <u>nothing</u> to do with the question. <u>Don't</u> write about every tiny little thing — only write about the bits that the <u>question</u> asks for.

Don't just scan this page — read it properly...

Scanning a text to find key words and phrases is a really important skill to learn — being able to do it well will save you bags of time in your exams. Every second counts, you know.

Writing Your Answer

Now you know how to pick out the important bits from a text, it's time to learn to write an answer.

Some questions ask you to **Find Facts**

Some questions will ask you to <u>find</u> a piece of <u>information</u> in the text.
Have a look at this example question:

 Which three countries did Katie and Nick visit on their holiday?   [3]

This question is asking you to find some <u>specific information</u> in the text...

— **Example** —

Katie and Nick visited Germany, Switzerland and Hungary on their holiday.

...so all you need to do in the answer is <u>provide</u> the
<u>facts</u> that the question is looking for to get your marks.

Some questions are a bit **Trickier**

Some questions want you to show whether you <u>understand</u>
how certain <u>effects</u> are <u>created</u> in the text:

 How does the writer try to make you feel sympathy for Mr Hill?   [6]

This question is asking you to think about <u>how</u> the <u>author</u> has
used <u>language</u> to make you <u>feel sympathy</u> for a character.

Use **P.E.E.** to write **Answers** to these questions

I'm not being silly. P.E.E. stands for: <u>Point</u>, <u>Example</u>, <u>Explanation</u>.
It's a great way to write an answer for these trickier types of question:

<u>Point</u>: Make a point that will <u>answer</u> the question.

<u>Example</u>: Give an example from the <u>text</u>.

<u>Explanation</u>: Show how the example <u>backs up</u> your point.

*Start a new paragraph every
time you make a new point.*

— **Example** —

This is your <u>example</u>
— a quotation from
the text.

Use <u>linking phrases</u>
like this when you
start your next point.

    The writer uses Mr Hill's past to make us feel
sympathy for him. We're told that Mr Hill "always
tried in vain" to please his father. This tells us that
his father was never happy with anything he did.
Another person who treats Mr Hill badly is his
supervisor at work. She is always telling him that...

This is your
<u>point</u>.

This bit is your
<u>explanation</u>.

First state the **Obvious**

1) You might read a question and think, "I can't think of <u>anything</u> clever to say."
    Don't worry — think of something <u>obvious</u> to say.

2) Sensible points will often be the right ones, even if they hardly seem worth saying at first.

3) If you notice something in the <u>text</u> that seems to answer the <u>question</u>,
    the chances are it <u>does</u>, so <u>write it down</u>.

4) <u>DON'T</u> think, "Oh, that's obvious, there's no point in putting that".
    Of course there's a point — the point is — <u>if it's right, write it down</u>.

Here's an example of making **Simple Points**

Look at this question and example answer:

> **Q** What does the writer tell us about Lee's
> feelings in the dentist's waiting room?   [3]

Lee shivered. He pulled his coat tightly around him, although it wasn't cold.
His fists were clenched in his pockets. He stared at the floor in front of his feet
and occasionally glanced nervously at the other people in the waiting room.

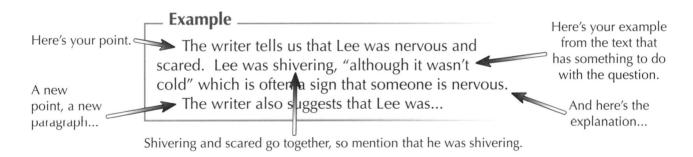

— **Example** —

Here's your point. → The writer tells us that Lee was nervous and scared. Lee was shivering, "although it wasn't cold" which is often a sign that someone is nervous.

Here's your example from the text that has something to do with the question.

A new point, a new paragraph... → The writer also suggests that Lee was...

And here's the explanation...

Shivering and scared go together, so mention that he was shivering.

This answer may sound <u>simple</u>, but if you don't <u>write it down</u> then the examiner will think that you didn't notice it.

One way to think about it is to <u>pretend the examiner isn't very clever</u> — imagine that you have to <u>explain everything</u> to them using <u>simple points</u>.

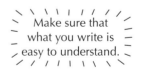
Make sure that what you write is easy to understand.

No one will think you're stupid for stating the obvious...

So it's like this: make a really simple point that's really obvious in the text, back it up with a little quotation from the text itself, then explain how it answers the question. It's as easy as P.E.E..

Summary Questions

Wa-hey — made it to the end of the section. Time for some Summary Questions... Not the most exciting things ever, but these ARE extremely useful. You can test your knowledge on how to answer reading questions and make sure you know all the tricks and techniques of the trade. If there's anything you're stuck on, go straight back over those pages, and get it learned.

1) What is the difference between setting and perspective?

2) Give two possible themes for a novel called "My Brother's Wedding".

3) What is the point of stage directions in a play?

4) How might imagining that you're a director help you when you're reading a play?

5) Rewrite this sentence to turn it into a cracking sentence from a piece of travel writing: "They saw a tower in front of a forest and they could not believe it."

6) What's the difference between a biography and an autobiography?

7) Why are biographies often biased (or one-sided)?

8) Name two different types of poem.

9) What is a group of lines in a poem called? Give both possible answers.

10) Why is it helpful to skim-read a text first, before you read it properly?

11) A key word is:
    a) always the first word in a sentence,
    b) a word that is important in understanding the meaning of a text, or
    c) a word that gets you into locked places.

12) How can 'scanning' help you to answer a question in your exam?

13) How would your answers to these two questions differ?
    a) Find three words which describe the mongoose.
    b) How does the poet try to make the reader dislike the mongoose?

14) What does P.E.E. stand for? (No funny business, mind.)

15) Which of the statements below is true?
    a) You should pretend that your examiner is a genius and not make any simple points, or
    b) You should pretend that your examiner isn't very clever, and make simple points and explain things clearly.

Choice of Vocabulary

Vocabulary is a just a fancy name for words. Writers have to choose their words carefully.

*Think about the text's **Purpose** and **Audience***

Different texts will use <u>different vocabulary</u> depending on what
the <u>purpose</u> of the text is and who the <u>audience</u> is. For example:

> The vocabulary used by a character in a play reflects their personality. It could be formal or informal, depending on the impression the writer wants to give.

> A piece of travel writing will use lots of descriptive vocabulary.

> I never really connected with my uncle. We just didn't get on. He was a stubborn fellow and made it clear that he didn't like me...

Informal language is the kind of language you use with <u>friends</u> or <u>family</u>. A writer might use it to give a <u>personal</u> account, e.g. in an <u>autobiography</u>.

Formal language is used for more <u>serious</u> stuff.
It's the type of language you might find in a <u>classic novel</u>.

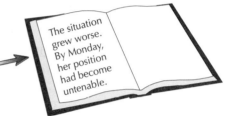

> The situation grew worse. By Monday, her position had become untenable.

*Slang makes a **Text** seem **Chatty***

1) Slang is <u>really informal</u> language.

2) Characters in <u>novels</u> or <u>plays</u> often use slang in their <u>dialogue</u> (when they're talking), as it makes speech sound more <u>natural</u>.

3) Some <u>informal texts</u> use slang to make the readers feel that the narrator is <u>chatting</u> to them. Here are some examples of slang:

> I needed some grub.

> "Cheers, mate!"

> We spotted the celebs in Coventry.

*Technical Language makes a text seem **Informative***

1) <u>Technical language</u> uses lots of specialist words that are <u>specific</u> to a certain topic. It shows that the writer <u>knows a lot</u> about that subject.

2) Sometimes a character or narrator will use technical language to make what they're saying seem more <u>persuasive</u>.

> Average worldwide temperatures have increased by about 1°C in the last hundred years, mainly due to increased emission of gases such as carbon dioxide.

This is an example of <u>technical</u> language. It uses <u>specialist terms</u> like 'emission' and 'carbon dioxide'.

Use yer crust — learn this blinder of a page...

When you're reading, bear in mind that writers are very picky when choosing the words for their texts. Ask yourself why they chose the words they did and what effect they wanted to achieve.

Figurative Language

Figurative language can have a very powerful effect on the reader. Read on to see how...

Figurative Language makes texts more Interesting

Figurative language makes a text more appealing and engaging.
Examples of figurative language include:

imagery   onomatopoeia   personification   exaggeration

similes   alliteration   metaphors

A Simile says something is Like something else

A simile is a way of describing something by saying it's like something else.
Similes usually use the words "as" or "like".

The thief crept up as quietly as a mouse.   ← This is a simile. It tells you how quiet the thief was.

I'd forgotten my gloves and soon my fingers were like blocks of ice.

This is a simile. It tells you how cold his fingers were.

A Metaphor says something Is something else

Metaphors describe something by saying that it is something else.
They never use 'like' or 'as'. For example:

Jeremy is a pig when he eats.

This is a metaphor. Jeremy isn't actually a pig, but it describes how Jeremy eats.

Imagery is about making a Picture

Imagery uses words to create a picture in the reader's mind.
Writers often use similes and metaphors to do this.

The desert stretched out before us, as white and as empty as the surface of the moon.

The strawberries were fragrant jewels, freshly picked and glistening.

Personification *is another kind of* Comparison

Personification is when something is described as if it's a person.

> The autumn leaves danced playfully in the wind.

Leaves can't actually dance, but it creates a nice image for the reader.

> The sun smiled on the people below.

This sounds like the sun has a human expression.

Writers Exaggerate *for* Effect

Exaggeration is when an unrealistic comparison is made for effect. It's also called hyperbole.

> Jack was as tall as a tree.

> Freda was as old as the hills.

Trees are pretty tall, and hills are pretty old, so these are good comparisons. You don't literally mean that Jack was as tall as a tree or Freda was as old as a hill — but people will understand.

Alliteration *is when* Sounds *are* Repeated

When lots of words start with the same sound, it's called alliteration.

> The acclaimed actors flocked to the famous film festival.

This sentence has two lots of alliteration.

When words contain the same vowel sound, it's called assonance.

Even though they're spelt differently, these vowel sounds are the same, so it's assonance.

> The game changed when we had the weight of eight men behind us.

Onomatopoeia — Sounds Like *what it's talking about*

Some words sound a bit like the noise they're talking about — this technique is called onomatopoeia. Writers use onomatopoeia to make their descriptions sound more effective.

> "Crunch" went Jamie's bike, as he smashed into the car.

> The car screeched to a halt.

This page is more helpful than a life jacket in a flood...

Maybe that's an exaggeration. But it's still pretty useful. If you want to sound like you know your stuff when you're writing about a text, learning these terms will be dead handy. Trust me.

Section Three — Reading: The Details

Mood

This isn't about someone having a sulk in the corner — it's about how a text makes you feel.

The **Mood** of a **Text** is how it makes you **Feel**

1) The writer uses <u>language</u> to <u>create the mood</u> in a piece of text.

2) A text can make us feel <u>happy</u>, <u>sad</u> or even <u>scared</u>... Boo!

Look for **Devices** that **Create** the **Mood**

1) When you read a text, look for <u>words</u> that make you feel a certain <u>emotion</u>. That will help you to work out the mood of the text.

   For example, the writer's language can create a <u>positive</u> or <u>happy</u> mood in the text.

   Words like 'jubilant' and 'triumphantly' create a <u>happy mood</u>.

   > Feeling jubilant, Kay let himself freewheel down the hill, the wind blowing triumphantly through his hair. The birds whistled in the trees, cheering him on. He grinned. He was going to win now, without a doubt.

   This is <u>personification</u>. It's used here to show how positive Kay feels.

2) Writers also use some <u>clever techniques</u> to build the mood. For example, <u>short words</u> and <u>short, sharp sentences</u> can create an atmosphere of <u>tension</u>.

   Words like 'suddenly' create a sense of <u>shock</u>.

   > Suddenly, the floorboard creaked. Prakash froze. His heart pounded in his chest. His blood turned to ice. He was going to be caught. He knew it.

   <u>Metaphors</u> can create images that add to the sense of <u>fear</u>.

   <u>Short sentences</u> add tension.

3) Another technique is using <u>ellipses</u> to create <u>suspense</u>:

   > Holding her breath, Lucy reached with trembling hands to stack the last two cards on the tower... If it fell now, all her hard work would be ruined...

   Ellipses create a <u>pause</u>, which can add suspense.

4) <u>Nothing</u> in a text is <u>accidental</u>. A writer <u>chooses</u> their words <u>deliberately</u> to make the readers feel happy, or sad, or tense, or excited, or whatever.

The way it makes me feel — it knocks me off my feet...

First off, learn these techniques that writers use to create a mood. Then try spotting them in the texts you read. It gets easier with practice, so get reading and I'm sure you'll be a pro in no time.

Characterisation

You need to learn how writers show their characters' personalities in their texts.

Writers tell you about their Characters

1) The way a writer gives the reader information about their characters is called <u>characterisation</u>.

2) You can <u>learn</u> about characters by what they <u>say</u> and <u>do</u>, what <u>other characters</u> say about them, and from their <u>own thoughts</u> and <u>feelings</u> (especially if the text is written in the <u>first person</u>).

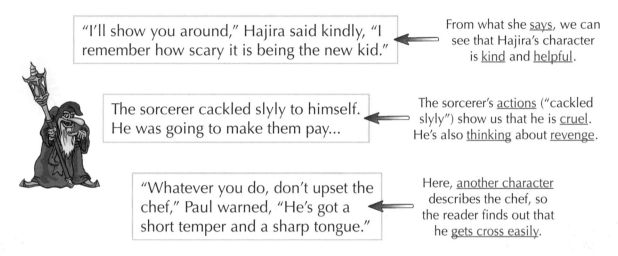

"I'll show you around," Hajira said kindly, "I remember how scary it is being the new kid."

From what she <u>says</u>, we can see that Hajira's character is <u>kind</u> and <u>helpful</u>.

The sorcerer cackled slyly to himself. He was going to make them pay...

The sorcerer's <u>actions</u> ("cackled slyly") show us that he is <u>cruel</u>. He's also <u>thinking</u> about <u>revenge</u>.

"Whatever you do, don't upset the chef," Paul warned, "He's got a short temper and a sharp tongue."

Here, <u>another character</u> describes the chef, so the reader finds out that he <u>gets cross easily</u>.

There are Different Types of Character

In stories and plays there are <u>different types</u> of character.
There can be <u>evil</u> characters, <u>good</u> characters, <u>funny</u> characters, etc...

Sometimes these different types of character can <u>stand</u> for certain <u>ideas</u>.
For example, a character could represent <u>love</u>, <u>evil</u> or <u>authority</u>.

A teacher could be used to represent wisdom.

A greedy businessman could represent corruption.

If I were a character, I would represent perfection...

Of course, some characters are not straightforward good or evil types. They can be a bit more complicated than that. But you should be able to spot the simple ones when they do crop up.

Irony and Symbolism

Sometimes you have to read between the lines of a text to discover its real meaning...

Irony can add Humour to texts

1) Irony is when someone <u>says one thing</u> but <u>means another</u>.
It can be used to <u>entertain</u> a reader by making the text <u>funnier</u>.

> What a great idea of mine to go for a nice long walk on the rainiest day of the year.

It's clear the narrator <u>doesn't</u> think it was a <u>great idea</u> to go for a walk on a particularly rainy day — it's <u>ironic</u>.

2) Something is ironic if there's a <u>big difference</u> between what people <u>expect</u> and what <u>actually happens</u>.

> Dr Foster ran across the road to avoid getting wet in the rain, but he tripped and fell into a puddle right up to his chin.

This is <u>ironic</u> because Dr Foster <u>thought</u> he'd get <u>less wet</u> by running across the road — <u>actually</u>, he got <u>more wet</u>.

3) Irony is often used to make texts more <u>interesting</u> and add <u>layers</u> of <u>meaning</u>.

> Water, water, everywhere,
> Nor any drop to drink.

In his poem, 'The Rime of the Ancient Mariner', Coleridge describes the <u>irony</u> of a stranded ship <u>surrounded by sea water</u>, but <u>without</u> a drop of water that the crew can <u>drink</u>.

Symbols give things a more Significant Meaning

1) You'll come across symbols in <u>everyday life</u>, e.g. a yawn symbolises someone being bored.

2) <u>Symbolism</u> is when <u>objects</u> or <u>actions</u> are used to signify <u>ideas</u> beyond what is <u>obvious</u>.

3) <u>Traditional</u> examples in literature include a <u>dove</u> symbolising <u>peace</u>, or a <u>red rose</u> symbolising <u>love</u>.

> My heart leaps up when I behold
> A rainbow in the sky:

In this poem, William Wordsworth uses the rainbow as a symbol of <u>hope</u>.

A literary cymbal? Sounds noisy and annoying...

That kind of cymbal won't help you in the exam, but knowing about the symbols on this page will. Make sure you know how irony and symbols are used to give texts extra layers of meaning.

Section Three — Reading: The Details

Poetry Conventions

Rhyming is pretty darn important in poems. Time to see how it all works...

Words **Rhyme** if their **Endings** sound the **Same**

Although poems <u>don't</u> have to rhyme, rhyme is used <u>a lot</u> so you need to <u>understand</u> how it works. Rhyming words are words that <u>sound</u> the same.

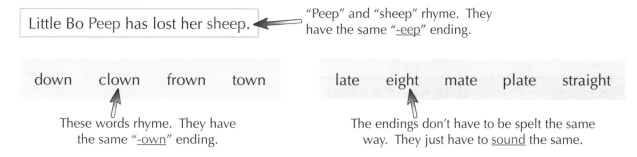

Little Bo Peep has lost her sheep.

"Peep" and "sheep" rhyme. They have the same "<u>-eep</u>" ending.

down   clown   frown   town

These words rhyme. They have the same "<u>-own</u>" ending.

late   eight   mate   plate   straight

The endings don't have to be spelt the same way. They just have to <u>sound</u> the same.

A **Rhyming Couplet** is **Two Lines** that rhyme

If a line of poetry <u>rhymes</u> with the <u>next</u> one, you've got a <u>rhyming couplet</u>.
Lots of poetry is made of rhyming couplets.

This is an extract from the poem 'The Land of Story-books' by Robert Louis Stevenson:

At evening when the lamp is lit,
Around the fire my parents sit;
They sit at home, and talk and sing,
And do not play at anything.

<u>Lit</u> rhymes with <u>sit</u>.

<u>Sing</u> rhymes with <u>thing</u>.

Here's another example from a nursery rhyme:

Ring a ring of roses
A pocket full of posies.

<u>Roses</u> rhymes with <u>posies</u>. (It isn't such an exact rhyme, this time.)

Repetition emphasises **Key Ideas**

Poets <u>repeat</u> words, <u>phrases</u>, and even <u>whole lines</u>, in order to <u>emphasise</u> points in their poems.
If you spot a word or phrase that's <u>repeated</u>, you can be sure that it's <u>important</u>...

These lines are from Robert Burns's poem, 'My Heart's in the Highlands'.

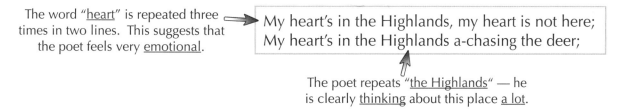

The word "<u>heart</u>" is repeated three times in two lines. This suggests that the poet feels very <u>emotional</u>.

My heart's in the Highlands, my heart is not here;
My heart's in the Highlands a-chasing the deer;

The poet repeats "<u>the Highlands</u>" — he is clearly <u>thinking</u> about this place <u>a lot</u>.

Rhythm *is important in* Poetry

A lot of poetry follows a <u>rhythm pattern</u>. There might be a fixed pattern of <u>syllables</u> on each line. If a line has <u>too many syllables</u>, it won't <u>fit</u> with the rest of the verse.

> Jack and Jill went up the hill,
> To fetch a pail of water.
> Jack fell down and broke his crown,
> While Jill stood at the top laughing at him for being so clumsy.

There are <u>far too many syllables</u> here...

A syllable is a part of a word that can be said in a single sound, e.g. 'family' has three syllables — 'fam-i-ly'.

Metre *means the* Rhythm *of a poem*

<u>Metre</u> is the name for the <u>rhythm</u> and <u>syllable pattern</u> of a poem.

A syllable is stressed if you emphasise it more, e.g. mag-a-ZINE, vol-CA-no, CU-cum-ber.

Some poetry has a <u>pattern</u> of stressed and unstressed syllables that mirrors normal speech. It gives poetry a very natural rhythm.

My mistress' eyes are nothing like the sun.

Sometimes this rhythm is <u>disrupted</u> to <u>emphasise</u> a particular word. Look at how Alexander Pope uses a <u>disrupted rhythm</u> to change the emphasis in this quotation.

To err is human; to forgive, divine.

Two <u>unstressed</u> syllables together disrupts the <u>flow</u> of the line — it puts the <u>focus</u> on 'forgive'. <u>Ending</u> on a <u>stressed</u> syllable gives the line a sense of <u>authority</u> and <u>certainty</u>.

You need to Think *about the poem's* Structure

A poem's <u>structure</u> is made up of its <u>lines</u>, <u>verses</u>, <u>rhyme pattern</u>, and <u>rhythm</u>. Some poems, like sonnets, have a <u>set structure</u>, e.g. most sonnets have 14 lines. Have a look at the structure of '<u>The Eagle</u>' by Alfred Lord Tennyson.

> He clasps the crag with crooked hands;
> Close to the sun in lonely lands,
> Ringed with the azure world, he stands.
>
> The wrinkled sea beneath him crawls;
> He watches from his mountain walls,
> And like a thunderbolt he falls.

This poem has <u>two verses</u> and each verse has <u>three lines</u>.

Each line has <u>eight syllables</u>.

Every line in each verse <u>rhymes</u>.

Read carefully, and you'll notice that every other syllable is <u>stressed</u>.

Metre — not a hundred centimetres...

Rhythm and metre are trickier than rhyme so re-read this page till they're both clear in your mind. Then cover the page and jot it all down from memory — you'll be a poetry whizz in no time.

Summary Questions

Finished these pages on reading? Feeling ready to go? Then go ahead and run through these questions. If any of them fox you, go back through this section until you find the answer.

1) An actor is playing a scientist in a play. He is explaining astrophysics.
   His lines will mostly use:
   a) simple, easy language   b) technical language   c) slang

2) List three figurative language techniques.

3) Decide whether the following sentences are similes or metaphors:
   a) The palms of her hands were sandpaper.
   b) He was a beast with the ball.
   c) The car was like an oven.
   d) The snow lay over the fields like a white blanket.

4) What is personification?

5) Which words in these sentences are examples of onomatopoeia?
   a) The snake hissed unhappily as they looked at it through the glass.
   b) They uncorked the bottle of champagne with a loud pop.
   c) The collection of tins clanged and clattered in the boot of the car.

6) What is the effect of using short words or short, sharp sentences in a text?
   a) It makes everyone laugh until their sides ache.
   b) It makes it seem more soppy and romantic.
   c) It helps create a feeling of tension.

7) Why do writers use ellipses?

8) The way a writer gives the reader information about their characters is called personalisation. True or false?

9) Which of these things help us to learn about characters?
   a) The things they say
   b) Their thoughts and feelings
   c) Their star signs
   d) Their baking abilities
   e) The things other characters say about them

10) What is irony?

11) Name something that could be used as a symbol of evil in a literary text.

12) Pair up the rhyming words:
    mane   gate   mine   plain   tea   see   straight   fine

13) A rhyming couplet is only made up of two lines. True or false?

14) Why might a poet repeat a word in a line or verse?

15) What is the difference between a stressed and an unstressed syllable?

16) Lara McLaughalot says, "A metre is a hundred centimetres.
    It's nothing to do with poetry." Explain why she is wrong.

Give Reasons

In this section, you'll be trained to give reasons for anything and everything...

Give **Reasons** from the **Text**

1) You have to give <u>reasons</u> for what you say by using <u>examples</u> from the passage you've read.

2) They show <u>where</u> your answer has <u>come from</u>.

3) If you <u>don't</u> give reasons, your answer won't show <u>you know</u> what you're talking about.

4) <u>Examples</u> show you haven't got it right by <u>lucky fluke</u>. Here's a handy example...

> **Example**
>
> The women at the book club aren't very friendly. In fact they're very rude.

 This answer <u>doesn't</u> give any reasons...

> **Example**
>
> The women at the book club are not very welcoming: they ignore Mrs Irvine when she tries to say hello. They even look at her and then start talking among themselves. This makes them seem very rude.

...but this answer gives a <u>reason</u> from the writing to justify every point it makes. That's loads better.

Every Time you make a **Point** — give an **Example**

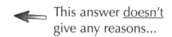

1) It's easy to <u>forget</u> to give examples from the bit of writing you've read. But your answer will make <u>more sense</u> and have a <u>clearer structure</u> if you give <u>proof for every point</u> you make.

2) It's best to <u>imagine</u> that the person reading your answers has <u>never seen the text</u> you're talking about.

3) Drum this <u>simple rule</u> into your head:

> <u>Every time</u> you make a <u>point</u>, <u>back it up</u> with an <u>example</u>.

Give reasons — and currants, and sultanas...

The sure-fire way to write really good responses and to prove your inner English genius is to cram loads of examples into your answer. Reasons and examples — keep 'em coming.

Using Your Own Words

When you link your answer to the piece you've read, use new words to show you understand it.

Don't just Copy bits out

When you give your answer, <u>don't</u> just <u>copy out</u> what the piece says, word for word.
Anyone can do that, so it <u>doesn't prove</u> that you've <u>understood</u> it.

Here's part of a story:

> Mrs Irvine began to introduce herself. But the sour-faced woman
> turned away and started to talk to her companions.

And here's a possible answer about it...

Don't be a Copy cat.

Example

> When Mrs Irvine began to introduce herself, the sour-faced
> woman turned away and started to talk to her companions.

> This <u>isn't</u> a good way to talk about the story.
> It uses all the <u>same words</u> as the story — it
> <u>doesn't</u> show that you actually <u>understand</u> it.

Put the reason in Your Own Words instead

Prove you've understood what you've read — use <u>your own words</u>.
Here is a <u>much better</u> answer about the bit of text above.

Example

> The woman ignored Mrs Irvine when she tried to introduce herself.

> This answer <u>paraphrases</u> the text above — it
> uses different words to say the same thing.

<u>Remember</u> — when you're giving a <u>reason</u>, always use <u>your own words</u>.

Tracing teeth marks? — Don't copy 'bites' out...

You know you have to give reasons and explanations in your answers and that means you've got
to use your own words. So kick-start your brain and say it your way — don't just copy it.

How to Quote

Your answer won't be complete if you don't stick in loads of lovely quotations...

Quote, Quote, Quote — and Quote some More

1) It's <u>not</u> a good idea to copy out what a piece says <u>word for word</u>, but <u>quoting</u> is a great way to <u>improve</u> your answer.

2) Quotations are great because they show <u>exactly</u> which bit you've got your answer from.

3) Quoting <u>isn't</u> the same as stealing words from the text you've read. There's a <u>massive difference</u>...

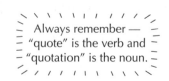

Always remember —
"quote" is the verb and
"quotation" is the noun.

Quotations have Speech Marks

<u>Speech marks</u> show that <u>you're quoting</u>, not stealing words. Here's an example:

> Mrs Irvine began to introduce herself. But the sour-faced woman turned away and began to talk to her companions. All the other women glanced briefly at Mrs Irvine.

Example

> The writer describes one of the women as "sour-faced". That makes us think she's not a nice person.

Everything inside the <u>speech marks</u> is a <u>quotation</u>. It has to be what the text says <u>word for word</u>.

Be careful you don't get confused between these two:

<u>Backing up</u> a point with a <u>reason</u> — use <u>your own words</u>.
<u>Backing up</u> a point with a quotation — <u>copy</u> that bit of text <u>exactly</u> and put it in <u>speech marks</u>.

Some quotations are a Bit Tricky

1) If you're quoting <u>more than one line</u> of <u>poetry</u>, put a '<u>/</u>' to show where a <u>new line</u> starts:

Example

> William Wordsworth, in his poem 'Daffodils', describes his happiness when he thinks about daffodils: "my heart with pleasure fills, / And dances with the daffodils".

2) If you're quoting from a <u>play</u>, you must make it clear <u>who's speaking</u>:

Example

> On line 7, Benedict claims that "Humphrey is as useful as an inflatable pincushion".

Quote early, quote often...

Everyone will love you if you quote bits from the text*. Remember copying is bad, quoting is good. Oh, and don't forget, quotations always have to have speech marks.   *Although I can't prove that point.

Explain the Quotation

You always have to make sure you explain why you're using a quotation.

Put the explanation **Before** the quotation

Here a quotation is used to <u>back up a reason</u> that's been given:

The answer <u>makes a point</u> — it says the women are rude.

Then there's <u>a reason to back it up</u> — the women talk among themselves even though they know Mrs Irvine is there.

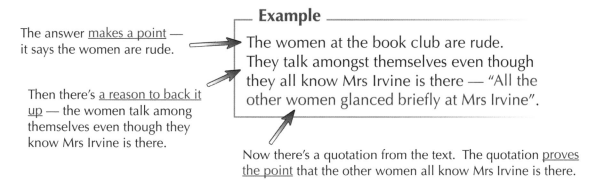

— **Example** —

The women at the book club are rude. They talk amongst themselves even though they all know Mrs Irvine is there — "All the other women glanced briefly at Mrs Irvine".

Now there's a quotation from the text. The quotation <u>proves the point</u> that the other women all know Mrs Irvine is there.

Or give the quotation **First**

Here a quotation is used <u>first</u>, and followed by an <u>explanation</u>.

Always explain why the quotation is relevant.

— **Example** —

The writer describes one of the women as "sour-faced". That makes us think she's not a nice person.

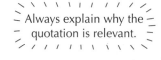

This time the quotation gets in there <u>first</u>. Then the answer explains why it's <u>relevant</u> to the point — that she isn't nice.

If you just wrote this bit, your answer <u>wouldn't</u> be entirely <u>complete</u> — you're not really making a point. You need to explain <u>why</u> you think the quotation is important or what its <u>effect</u> is in the text.

The writer describes one of the women as "sour-faced".

It <u>doesn't matter</u> what order you do it in — make a point, then back it up with a quotation — or quote then explain. The important thing is that you <u>always explain why</u> your quotation <u>helps</u> your <u>point</u>.

What came first, the quotation or the explanation...

Well, it doesn't really matter. But remember, you know why you chose your quotation. Only you. No one else will know (except maybe some talented psychics). So make sure you tell them.

Keeping Quotations Short

Keep your quotations short and sweet — mega-long quotations can confuse readers...

Never quote more than a *Few Words*...

Quotations show that <u>you've read</u> and <u>understood</u> the <u>text</u> you're talking about. You usually only need to quote a few words. Look at this example from 'Porphyria's Lover' by Robert Browning.

— **Example** —————————

Browning creates a tense atmosphere by describing
a brutal storm with human characteristics:
"The rain set early in tonight,
  The sullen wind was soon awake,
  It tore the elm-tops down for spite,
  And did its worst to vex the lake:
  I listened with heart fit to break."

This quotation is <u>far too long</u>. If your quotations are muddled, you'll sound <u>unsure</u>. Extra-long quotations could also <u>confuse</u> your reader.

— **Example** —————————

Browning creates a tense
atmosphere by describing
a brutal storm with human
characteristics:
"The sullen wind was
soon awake".

This quotation is loads <u>better</u>. It's <u>short</u> and it has everything you need to make your <u>point</u>.

Here's another example from Rupert Brooke's poem, 'The Soldier':

— **Example** —————————

The poet tries to find comfort in the idea of dying at war:
"And think, this heart, all evil shed away,
  A pulse in the eternal mind, no less
  Gives somewhere back the thoughts by England given;
  Her sights and sounds; dreams happy as her day;
  And laughter, learnt of friends; and gentleness,
  In hearts at peace, under an English heaven."

This one is an entire <u>verse</u> — that's <u>way too long</u>.

— **Example** —————————

The poet tries to find
comfort in the idea of dying
at war when he writes about
"hearts at peace, under an
English heaven."

This quotation is much <u>better</u> — it just uses a <u>few words</u> to make the point.

Try to quote using the <u>fewest</u> number of words you can.
Don't be afraid to quote a <u>single word</u> if it's <u>enough</u> to make your point.

...but do it **Often**

Your answer should be <u>full</u> of <u>short</u> quotations <u>backing up</u> your points.

You might not always be able to find the exact quotation you're looking for — but your answers will be better with a selection of <u>good quotations</u>.

Quotations — keep 'em short and sweet.

Phew-urgh words are better...

You don't need to quote vast chunks of writing, just the bit that makes the point. It's quicker, too.

Summary Questions

By now you should know everything there is to know about quoting. Lucky you. Remember, there's no way of creating the perfect answer without a clear and thorough understanding of the whole of this section. And there's an easy way to work out if you've got to grips with it — test yourself on these questions, and go over the section until you can do them all. Instantly. No hesitation. Like a pro.

1) What do you have to do to back up every point you make?

2) Complete this simple rule:
   "Every time you make a point, _____ it _____ with an _____."

3) A good way to remember to back up your point is to:
   a) imagine that your reader is an expert on the text you're talking about,
   b) imagine that your reader has never seen the text you're talking about, or
   c) imagine that you're a field agent calling for backup.

4) When you give your answer, why shouldn't you write your reasons in exactly the same words as the original piece of writing?

5) When can you copy the words of a text exactly?

6) How do you show that something's a quotation?

7) Complete the sentences below.
   a) When you back up a point with a _____, you must use your own words.
   b) When you back up a point with a _____, you must copy that bit of text exactly.

8) If you're quoting more than one line of poetry, when should you use this '/' symbol?

9) What do you need to make sure you do when quoting from a play?

10) What are the two ways in which you can give a reason and explain it with a quotation?

11) Give one reason why quotations shouldn't be too long.

12) How often should you use quotations?

The Writing Section

We met the reading exam in Section 2. Now it's time to tackle its mate — the writing exam.

Both exams have a Writing Section

As you might know by now, whether you're doing Level 1 or 2, there are two papers for the 13+ English exam. Each exam has a Section A and a Section B. Section B of both exams is the writing part.

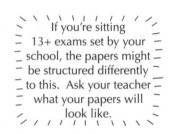

> If you're sitting 13+ exams set by your school, the papers might be structured differently to this. Ask your teacher what your papers will look like.

> In Paper 1, Section B, there'll be a choice of topics for you to write a text on — the questions could ask you to write a text in the form of a speech, a letter or an essay. See Section Six (p.38-46) for more information on the types of text that you might have to write.

> In Paper 2, Section B, you'll be asked to choose from a list of topics or titles, and write a descriptive or imaginative text. The question might ask you to write a short story (p.34), description or essay (p.33).

If you're doing the Common Academic Scholarship Examination, see p.55 for more information on its writing questions.

Spend 35 Minutes on the Writing Section

1) Each paper lasts 1 hour 15 minutes.

2) Each paper is worth 50 marks — 25 marks for the reading section and 25 marks for the writing section.

3) That means you'll have roughly 35 minutes for the writing section, with 5 minutes left at the end to check your work for mistakes.

4) In the writing section, you have a choice of several topics, but you only have to answer one question.

5) Make sure you spend a few minutes planning your work (see p.30). It'll help you to structure your answer well.

Spelling, Punctuation and Grammar are Important

1) The examiner will be looking out for some top-notch spelling, punctuation, grammar and vocabulary.

2) You need to work quickly in the exam, but make sure that you're careful to spell words correctly, punctuate your sentences well, and use paragraphs properly.

3) The examiner would love to see some exciting vocabulary in your answer too, so if you know a great word or phrase that would fit, then make sure you use it.

---

35 minutes, 25 marks — you do the maths...

Actually, don't worry about the maths — focus on the English. This section is all about how you can get some cracking marks in the writing section of your 13+ English exam. Ready? Let's go...

Looking at the Question

You're not going to write a decent answer if you don't look carefully at the question first.

Read *the* Question

It's always tempting to <u>start writing</u> straight away, but it's <u>not</u> a good idea.

1) Take the time to <u>read the question</u> and <u>think</u> about what it's asking you to do.

2) Make sure you know <u>what</u> you're supposed to write about before you get going.

Write in the *Style* that the *Question* tells you

Always think about what <u>kind of writing</u> the question is asking you to do. For example, you might be asked to imagine you're someone else, such as a teacher, or a character in a story. You have to think about what words <u>they would use</u> when they write or say something.

> Philip stood in the museum looking at the dinosaur bones. There was a sign saying, "Do not touch", but Philip didn't see it. After a while he reached out and grabbed hold of a bone. The museum attendant quickly ran over and told him to stop.

 Q Imagine you are the museum attendant. Write an account of the same event.

In this question, you're a <u>museum attendant</u>. You should write in the way that he or she would write, e.g. you might be <u>angry</u> about children mucking around in the museum.

— **Example** —
Children have no respect for the rules of the museum. Only today I had to stop a young boy from touching the dinosaur bones.

The style of your writing will depend on <u>who</u> you're writing to, <u>why</u> you're writing, and what <u>kind of text</u> a question is asking you to write.

If the question tells you to write a speech, be <u>snappy</u>, <u>punchy</u> and <u>direct</u> to get the reader's attention — like this.

— **Example** —
The faulty pelican crossing has caused ten accidents. We must take action now before someone else is injured, or even killed. Write to your local councillor at once.

If you're asked to write a formal letter of complaint, use loads of <u>formal language</u>, and don't forget to end it with 'Yours sincerely' or 'Yours faithfully' (see p.32 for which to use).

— **Example** —
Dear Mr Goodman,

    I am writing to complain about the appalling service that I experienced whilst dining at your restaurant. My wife and I were most distressed as we had to wait two hours for our meals...

Forget the hocus pocus — focus on the question...

It may sound an obvious thing to say, but reading the question carefully is incredibly important. No matter how good your answer is, if it doesn't do what the question asks you, it's no good.

Planning Your Answer

If you don't think planning is important, think again. A good plan can mean better writing.

Plan *before you start* Writing

If you <u>dive straight in</u> without planning first, it'll all go <u>horribly wrong</u>.

<u>One</u> page of well <u>planned</u>, well-thought-out writing is <u>always</u> better than <u>five</u> pages written off the <u>top</u> of your <u>head</u>.

Have a <u>good think</u> about what you're going to write about <u>before</u> you start. You don't need to know <u>exactly</u> what you're going to write, but you need to have a <u>rough idea</u>.

Good writing <u>makes a point</u>. It doesn't just ramble on about nothing.

Whether you're writing a story, a description, a letter or a speech, make sure you've got <u>enough different ideas</u> for the whole thing — no waffle.

Jot Down *your* Points *into a* Rough Plan

It's a good idea to jot down a <u>plan</u> of the points you want to make <u>before</u> you start writing. That way you won't get to the end and realise you've <u>forgotten</u> something.

> **Q** Write an article for a magazine about an issue that's important to you. Explain why you think the issue is important.

1) A plan doesn't have to be in proper sentences. It's just a <u>reminder</u> for you to use.

2) <u>Start</u> with what you think is the <u>most important</u> point. This grabs your reader's attention.

3) Try to <u>link</u> your points together. You can link smoothly from meat to treatment of animals.

4) Work out how you're going to <u>end</u> your piece. This is a positive ending — it says what we can do.

Example

Plan: Modern farming methods.

Reducing quality of soil — less food can be grown — soon we won't have enough to eat.

Risks to human health — pesticides — antibiotics in meat.

Animals treated badly — profits more important than welfare.

What we can do — buy organic.

No rambling — so no walking boots needed...

Without a plan, it's easy to let your writing ramble on. Always work out a plan before you put pen to paper. Before long, it will become second nature and your writing will be crazy good.

Section Five — Writing: The Basics

Structuring Your Writing

All writing follows a similar structure — it'll have a beginning, a middle and an end.

A *Good Introduction* is *Crucial*

An introduction is <u>really important</u>. A good one will make your reader want to <u>read on</u>.

Example

Do you ever dream of a better bed? If your current bed is old, hard or lumpy, it could be stopping you from getting the good night's sleep you deserve.

This is the introduction to a <u>persuasive</u> text that's trying to <u>sell</u> something. It uses a <u>question</u> to get the reader's attention and it makes the reader <u>feel important</u>.

This is the introduction to an argument. It sets out the <u>argument</u> clearly and uses <u>strong language</u> to convince the reader.

Example

I passionately believe that our school needs a breakfast club. Breakfast is the most important meal of the day. Research has proved time and time again that a good breakfast does wonders for our brains and our bodies.

Signposting sets out *What* you're going to *Say*

An introduction, especially in an <u>essay</u> or a <u>speech</u>, should set out what you're going to cover in the rest of the text. This is called <u>signposting</u>.

Example

Choosing to live a healthier life doesn't need to be complicated. There are three simple things you can do to improve your health: eat more fruit and vegetables, exercise regularly and eat less junk food.

This introduction <u>clearly</u> sets out <u>what</u> the text is going to cover and in <u>what order</u>. This way the reader knows exactly what they're going to find in the text.

The *Middle* is the *Main Bit* of your writing

The <u>middle bit</u> of your writing covers the main part of <u>what you want to say</u>. It should include all the things from your <u>plan</u> (see p.30) and follow the <u>order</u> that you set out in the <u>introduction</u>.

The main bit of your writing should be in <u>clear paragraphs</u>. Use a paragraph for each point (see p.59-61).

If you're writing to <u>inform</u>, <u>argue</u> or <u>persuade</u>, you should include some <u>facts</u> and <u>statistics</u> to support what you're saying.

Example

Fruit and vegetables contain lots of vitamins and nutrients that keep our bodies healthy...

Regular exercise is great for your heart and it can be loads of fun too...

Junk food is normally high in fat and sugar. Too much fat and sugar in your diet is bad for your health...

A **Good Ending** will **Impress** your reader

1) The ending is the <u>last thing</u> your reader will read, so you want it to be memorable.

2) If it's really good, it'll give your reader a <u>positive impression</u> of everything you've already said.

3) If you're writing to <u>argue</u> or <u>persuade</u>, then your ending is your <u>last chance</u> to get your reader to agree with you, so you've got to make it <u>first class</u>.

Different Texts need **Different Kinds** of **Ending**

Fiction texts need endings that <u>tie up the plot</u>, while non-fiction texts need <u>conclusions</u>.

Ending a **Story**

A good ending <u>ties up the loose ends</u> of the story. The reader shouldn't be left confused about what's happened.

If you write a story about a <u>personal experience</u> you could end it by saying how you feel about it now.

Example

Looking back, I feel lucky that nothing really bad happened to me. I still walk home, but I have never taken that short cut again.

Ending a **Letter**

1) For a formal letter, if you <u>know the name</u> of the <u>recipient</u>, end it with '<u>Yours sincerely</u>'.

2) If you <u>don't know</u> the name of the recipient, end the letter with '<u>Yours faithfully</u>'. You would do this if you addressed the letter '<u>Dear Sir</u>', like when writing to a <u>company</u>.

Example

I hope that you will resolve the issue as soon as possible. ◄——— Yours faithfully,

It's a good idea to end a <u>letter</u> of complaint by reminding the reader that they're supposed to <u>do something</u>.

Ending a **Persuasive Text** or **Speech**

A clever trick is to write a sentence in your conclusion that <u>links</u> to what you said in your <u>introduction</u>. You could also finish by asking the reader to <u>do something</u>.

Example — Introduction

The lack of facilities is an issue which affects us all. ⇒

Example — Conclusion

This is indeed an issue that affects us all. Please petition your local MP today.

Time to wrap it up — who's got the parcel tape?

A catchy beginning, a clear middle and a memorable ending — it sounds like a tall order. But follow the advice in this section, and with plenty of practice you'll soon be writing masterpieces...

Writing Essays

Have no fear — essays are no problem if you can keep your head and remember the basics.

Essays *Aren't Scary*

1) The word 'essay' sounds a bit scary. People tend to think that there's some great secret to writing essays — but it's just not true.

2) There will be an essay-style question on both of the writing papers — go back to p.28 for more information on the exams.

> An essay is a piece of writing that answers a question.
>
> A simple yes or no might answer the question — but it won't make a good essay — you need to explain why.

Three Steps *to essay Heaven*

Writing an essay is as easy as 1, 2, 3... (Well, not quite, but these steps will help.)

1) Think of some points to do with the question. See if you can use them to answer the question, then work out what order to put them in. This is your plan.

2) Style is important — write clearly and try to sound intelligent. Use posh clever-sounding words if you can, but only if you know what they mean.

3) Write about each point one at a time. When you write the essay, start a new paragraph each time you start a new point.

If you get an essay to write that isn't a direct question, turn it into a question:

> **Q** Write an essay about your favourite sport.

Turn the essay into this question:

> **Q** Why is your favourite sport good to play and fun to watch?

All you have to do is:

1) Think of reasons why it's a good sport for people to play, and write about them.

2) Think of reasons why it's fun to watch, and write about them too.

Essay? — No sweat...

Keep your cool and focus on what the question wants you to do. A good plan will help you to write your essay in clear, structured points, which is what the examiner will be looking for.

Writing Stories

It's not just essays that need plans. Stories improve with planning too.

Plan what will Happen in your Story

It's tempting just to start by writing "Once upon a time..." and hope that you'll be able to make up what happens in your story as you go along. But that's a really bad idea.

Before you start to write your story, you should have a good idea of how it's going to end, and what's going to happen in the middle. Otherwise you'll have all sorts of problems.

> Write about an exciting journey you have made. It can be real or imaginary.

Example

Plan: Going on holiday on a plane. ⟵ — This plan is like a summary of the story you're going to write.

Everyone except me got very ill from the food.

Went to the cockpit — pilot was unconscious. ⟵ — When you write the story, you could have two or three paragraphs about each of these points.

I talked to air traffic control over the pilot's radio and they told me what to do.

I landed the plane safely.

Everyone went to hospital — they were all fine. ⟵ — You've planned how it's going to end, so you always know what you're aiming towards.

Start with something Exciting

No one wants to read a story with a boring start. The beginning needs to GRAB THE READER'S ATTENTION. Start with something exciting, and the person reading your story can't help but want to read on. They'll want to find out what happens next.

Example

Naomi moved away. The edge of the cliff crumbled and she plunged backwards.

If you start with someone speaking, the person reading your story will want to find out who they are and what they're talking about.

Example

"Don't leave!" I cried, but the rocket was already taking off. Without it, I had no way of getting back to Earth.

You don't need to explain everything at once. Make the reader want to read on.

Grab 'em right at the start — then don't let 'em go...

It'll be loads easier for you to write a story if you already know exactly what's going to happen and how it's going to end. Otherwise, you run a serious risk of waffling — which is never good.

Section Five — Writing: The Basics

Correcting Mistakes

If you spot a mistake, don't panic — you'll know what to do once you've read this stuff...

Cross Out your mistakes Neatly

1) Don't worry if you find a <u>mistake</u> when you <u>check</u> your work. As long as your corrections are <u>clear</u>, you won't lose any marks.

2) If it's just <u>one word</u> or a <u>short phrase</u> that's wrong, cross it out <u>neatly</u> and write the <u>correct</u> word above it.

3) Always cross out the <u>whole word or phrase</u>, not just the wrong letters.

4) You should never write on top of a word to correct it — it's much <u>clearer</u> if you cross out the old word and write the new word <u>above</u>.

Don't use correction fluid or eraser pens — they look messy.

─ Example ─

The author uses a series of metafors to describe the rain.

Here's the <u>mistake</u> you need to <u>correct</u>.

─ Example ─

The author uses a series of met<del>af</del>ors to describe the rain.

Your writing won't be <u>clear</u> if you write <u>over</u> what you've already written.

─ Example ─

The author uses a series of _{metaphors} <del>metafors</del> to describe the rain.

This is <u>better</u> — draw a <u>clear line</u> through your mistake and write the <u>whole word</u> above it.

Always make sure the examiner can read your writing.

Use a Double Strike to show a New Paragraph

If you've <u>forgotten</u> to start a <u>new paragraph</u>, use a <u>double strike</u> (like this '///') to show where the new paragraph should begin.

You usually show the <u>start</u> of a <u>paragraph</u> with a <u>new line</u> and an <u>indent</u>.

Each new point needs a new paragraph. Your plan should show where each one starts.

─ Example ─

Our community garden is an important place where people of all ages can relax and enjoy nature in a safe environment. We believe that the garden should be given £200 so that we can purchase a brand new bench. //Another organisation that deserves money from the council is the local sports club. They want to build a new indoor tennis centre so that people can play tennis throughout the year.

Use a <u>double strike</u> to show that a <u>new paragraph</u> should <u>start</u> here.

Use an *Asterisk* to add *Extra Information*

If you realise that you've <u>missed something out</u>, the first thing to do is decide whether there's enough <u>space</u> to write the missing bit <u>above</u> the line you've already written.

If you <u>can</u>, write the missing bit <u>above</u> the line with a '∧' to show <u>exactly where</u> it should go.

> ### Example
>
> was
> The door creaked open, but there ∧nobody there.

This shows that the word 'was' is <u>missing</u> after 'there'.

If the bit you've missed out <u>won't</u> fit <u>above</u> the line, use an <u>asterisk</u> (like this *) to show <u>where</u> it should go. Write the missing stuff at the <u>end</u> of your essay with an asterisk next to it.

The <u>asterisk</u> shows that something is <u>missing</u> here.

> ### Example
>
> Brenda sprinted towards the station, but it was too late. * She turned back towards home, frustrated, and with David's brown leather briefcase still in her hand.

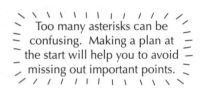

Too many asterisks can be confusing. Making a plan at the start will help you to avoid missing out important points.

> * David was already sitting on a train, hurtling through the countryside.

Put the asterisk <u>next to</u> the words you want to <u>add</u>.

Cross Out anything you *Don't* want to be *Marked*

If you don't want the examiner to read something, just <u>cross it out neatly</u>.

The same goes for parts of your answer that you decide are <u>wrong</u> — if you want to get rid of a <u>paragraph</u> in the middle of your answer, cross it out <u>clearly</u>. You can <u>replace</u> it with a new paragraph using an <u>asterisk</u> and a <u>new paragraph</u> at the end.

Try not to cross out too much stuff — you might get marks for some of it.

Always make sure your answers are clear and tidy.

Whatever you do, <u>don't</u> start <u>scribbling</u> things out willy nilly. It'll make your answer look really <u>messy</u>.

Correct me if I'm wrong, but this seems important...

Why yes it is — thank you ever so much for saying so. The main thing to remember is that everyone makes mistakes, but you'll do well if you can correct your mistakes clearly and neatly.

Summary Questions

You wouldn't think there were so many tricks to doing something as simple as writing, but trust me — knowing all the stuff in this section will make a huge difference. Just don't be a bird-brain and think you can wing it. Go over this section till you can answer every one of these questions.

1) What should you do instead of starting to write straight away at the start of an exam?

2) Explain what kind of style you would write in if you were each of these people:
   a) a headmaster   b) a rap musician   c) an author of a romantic novel

3) A speech should be: a) long and rambling   b) punchy and direct   c) in a foreign language

4) Which of these are good ideas for writing a plan for your answer?
   a) Always write in full sentences.
   b) Start with the most important point.
   c) Start with the least important point.
   d) Try to link your points together in a smooth argument.
   e) Don't bother with planning an ending — it'll probably change anyway.

5) It's a good idea to signpost your arguments in the: a) introduction b) conclusion.

6) When making your main points, you shouldn't bother following the order that you laid out in the introduction.
   True or false?

7) A text that aims to inform the reader contains:
   a) long, elegant descriptions,
   b) lots of facts, or
   c) lots of your own opinions.

8) How should you end a formal letter in the following situations?
   a) When you know the name of the recipient.
   b) When you don't know the name of the recipient.

9) It's a really effective idea to link the conclusion of your persuasive writing with:
   a) something you said in your introduction,
   b) something you said to your grandma last Tuesday, or
   c) something your mates have written in their essays.

10) What can you do to help you write an essay that isn't a direct question
    (e.g. Q: Write an essay about recycling in the UK)?

11) When you're planning a story, is it best to:
    a) not plan the ending, so you can decide at the last minute what you want to do, or
    b) plan the ending so you know what you're aiming towards?

12) Your story should begin with:
    a) a brief summary of the characters and plot,
    b) something exciting, or
    c) a long speech from the main character about what they had for lunch.

13) What can you do if you've forgotten to start a new paragraph?

14) What would you use an asterisk for in your answer?

Writing to Persuade and Argue

It's quite likely that you'll have to write a text in favour of an opinion, or to persuade someone.

Arguing and *Persuading* are quite similar

1) Writing to <u>argue</u> is about getting people to <u>agree with your opinions</u> and showing why other people's opinions are <u>wrong</u> (or at least not as good as yours).

2) Writing to <u>persuade</u> is when you encourage the reader to <u>do something</u> or to think in the <u>same way</u> you do. Persuading can be a lot like trying to <u>sell</u> something.

3) When you're writing to argue or persuade, you need to give <u>clear</u> and <u>convincing</u> reasons to support what you say. The techniques on the following pages are useful for both <u>arguing</u> and <u>persuading</u> — so learn them well.

Work out the **Opposite** *view — then say it's* **Wrong**

If you're trying to <u>persuade</u> someone to do something or <u>argue</u> an opinion, it's useful to look at it from <u>the other point of view</u>.

Think about why people might <u>not</u> agree with you — then work out how to <u>prove them wrong</u>.

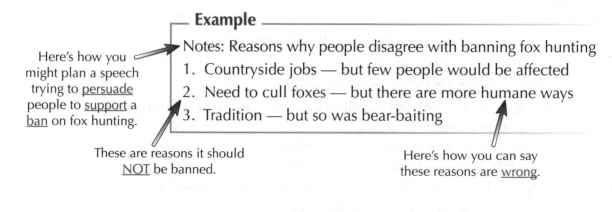

Here's how you might plan a speech trying to <u>persuade</u> people to <u>support</u> a <u>ban</u> on fox hunting.

---- **Example** --

Notes: Reasons why people disagree with banning fox hunting
1. Countryside jobs — but few people would be affected
2. Need to cull foxes — but there are more humane ways
3. Tradition — but so was bear-baiting

These are reasons it should <u>NOT</u> be banned.

Here's how you can say these reasons are <u>wrong</u>.

And here's how you could write out one of those points.

---- **Example** --

<u>Why fox hunting should be banned</u>
   Supporters of fox hunting say that it's a tradition.
But in the past, it was also traditional to bait bears.
Times change, and society moves on. Just because
something is traditional is no reason to keep doing it.

Show that you've <u>thought</u> about what your opponents say and that you still <u>disagree</u> with them. That way you'll have more chance of <u>convincing</u> other people that <u>your</u> view is <u>right</u>.

Exaggerate your **Good Points**

It might sound a bit <u>unfair</u> to exaggerate how good your own arguments are. But <u>don't worry</u> — everyone does it. If you don't exaggerate, people might think your points are <u>weak</u>.

This works really well in <u>articles</u>, <u>speeches</u>, and also in texts that are trying to <u>sell</u> a product.

Make your points with style, and use a few <u>facts</u> and <u>statistics</u> to make them more convincing.

___ **Example 1 — Rubbish** ___

Global warming could be quite a problem. Some scientists think the earth is getting warmer quite quickly. That might mean that a fair bit of farmland turns into desert, so people might not have enough food.

Words like "<u>massive</u>", "<u>frightening</u>" and "<u>huge</u>" are stronger than words like "quite" or "a fair bit".

It says "<u>many scientists</u>" instead of "some".

It says "<u>will</u>" and "<u>huge areas</u>" instead of "might" and "a fair bit".

It talks about "<u>billions</u> of people" instead of just saying "people".

Using "<u>starve</u>" is scarier than "not have enough food".

___ **Example 2 — Good** ___

Global warming is a massive threat to the very future of humanity. Many scientists believe the earth is getting warmer at a frightening rate. If this continues, huge areas of farmland will turn into desert, causing billions of people to starve.

Be careful, though — you're allowed to exaggerate, but you're <u>not</u> allowed to <u>lie</u>. You <u>can't</u> say things that <u>aren't true</u>, like "global warming will cause aliens to take over the Earth".

If you say things that <u>obviously aren't true</u>, people won't trust the rest of your arguments.

Make your **Opponents** sound **Unreasonable**

Putting your opponents' point of view in your own words is a good way of making them sound bad.

You can also <u>exaggerate</u> what people who disagree say, to make them sound <u>unreasonable</u>. It's a great tactic when writing an argument...

___ **Example** ___

Some businessmen believe we have no responsibility to the environment. They think it doesn't matter if we keep on churning out deadly greenhouse gases. All they care about is making profits.

You can be <u>harsh</u> — as long as you don't <u>tell any actual lies</u>.

___

10 out of 10 for exagge — a high exagge-rating...

Exaggeration is a crucial trick when you're arguing or persuading. You can use it to make yourself sound good, and make your opponents sound bad. But make sure you don't lie.

Section Six — Types of Writing

Writing to Explain

Writing to explain means giving people an explanation. It's not rocket science.

Explanations *tell your audience* **Five Main Things**

If you're writing to <u>explain</u>, you basically want your readers to <u>understand</u> as much as possible about your topic. Start by making sure you cover these <u>five key points</u>:

The WHAT...	...the HOW...	...the WHERE...
<u>What</u> is going on?	<u>How</u> is it happening?	<u>Where</u> is it happening?

...the WHEN..	...and the WHY.
<u>When</u> is it happening?	<u>Why</u> is it happening?

Explanations *can take* **Many Forms**

When you explain something, <u>break down the detail</u> of a topic to present it <u>clearly</u>. Just like revision, things are easier to understand when explained in smallish chunks.

Think carefully about <u>who</u> your writing is <u>aimed at</u> and <u>adapt</u> your writing style to this <u>audience</u>.

Here are some <u>examples</u> of "writing to explain" questions that could be in your exam:

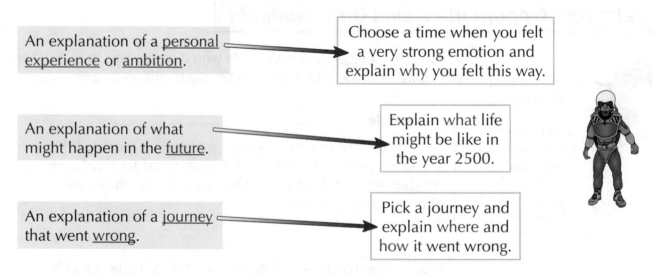

An explanation of a <u>personal</u> <u>experience</u> or <u>ambition</u>. → Choose a time when you felt a very strong emotion and explain why you felt this way.

An explanation of what might happen in the <u>future</u>. → Explain what life might be like in the year 2500.

An explanation of a <u>journey</u> that went <u>wrong</u>. → Pick a journey and explain where and how it went wrong.

What? Why? How? Is this some sort of investigation?

When you're writing to explain, make a list of the main points of information you want to cover before you start. It'll make it a lot easier to structure your answer and make it interesting.

Writing to Inform

When you write to inform, you do what it says on the tin — you give people information.

Writing to inform **Tells** the reader **Facts**

If you're writing to <u>inform</u>, you need to <u>tell</u> the reader
something as <u>clearly</u> and <u>effectively</u> as possible.

This might involve talking about <u>personal experiences</u> (e.g. a <u>significant incident</u> in
your life) or something you <u>feel strongly</u> about. You must make sure that you keep the
emphasis on giving out <u>clear facts</u> in an organised structure. Avoid opinions or waffle.

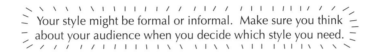
Your style might be formal or informal. Make sure you think
about your audience when you decide which style you need.

Informative language is **Clear** and **Factual**

1) Informative writing needs to be <u>snappy</u> and <u>direct</u>.

2) Make sure you stick to the <u>facts</u> and keep things <u>impersonal</u>.

3) Try and keep your sentences as <u>short</u> and as <u>straightforward</u> as possible.

Example

I reckon global warming is a big problem, as
it causes loads of environmental problems.

◄ This answer is too
personal. It's also really
vague and rambling.

Example

Global warming has led to a rise in the Earth's average temperature.
Consequences of this include droughts, hurricanes, fires and rising sea levels.

◄ This is loads
better.

There are **Loads** of **Examples** of **Writing to Inform**

Here are some different <u>types</u> of writing that you might be asked to do for an <u>inform</u> question.

A <u>letter</u> to a pen-friend telling
them about where you live.

An information <u>leaflet</u>
for a local museum.

A <u>personal account</u> of a
school or club event.

A <u>magazine article</u> informing people
about environmental problems.

Well, that all seems very informative...

Writing to inform is easy as long as you don't get over-excited. Your language should be calm
and factual. Avoid giving opinions and stick to a clear structure. Don't make things personal.

Writing to Advise

When you're writing to advise, you want to help the reader with some gems of wisdom.

There are many different **Types** of **Advice**

From 'how to quit smoking' leaflets to agony aunt pages, written advice is <u>everywhere</u>.

Writing to advise is a bit <u>weird</u> — it's a <u>mixture</u> of writing to <u>inform</u> and writing to <u>persuade</u>. For example, a leaflet on quitting smoking needs to <u>persuade</u> people to <u>quit</u> and <u>inform</u> them <u>how</u> to do it.

You could be asked to write any of these types of advice:

MAGAZINE AND NEWSPAPER ARTICLES e.g. how to eat a healthy diet
SPEECHES e.g. to advise pupils how to revise for exams effectively
MAGAZINE FEATURES e.g. a page about how to look after guinea pigs

Written advice needs to be **Reassuring**

1) Written advice has got to get the <u>reader's attention</u> — a good <u>heading</u> would do the trick.

2) It's got to be <u>clear</u> what the advice is <u>about</u> (e.g. from the heading) so that people can decide whether or not they want to read it. A leaflet on healthy eating is no good if it <u>looks</u> like a leaflet on bike maintenance...

3) Finally, if the reader is going to take your advice, they need to feel that you <u>understand</u> the issue thoroughly. You can convince them by using a <u>reassuring</u> tone throughout the text:

Great Exam Advice

> **Example**
>
> Don't worry if it takes a while for leaves to appear on the shoots — plants all grow at different rates. Just make sure you keep them well watered.

Written advice suggests what **Action** to take

So... when you're writing your advice, you need to get the reader's <u>attention</u>, <u>reassure</u> them about what they're doing, and then, finally, you can actually give them your <u>advice</u>.

You need to suggest to the reader what <u>courses of action</u> they could take.

You could give them a <u>range</u> of different <u>options</u> so they have some <u>choice</u>.

Then it's all up to the <u>reader</u> to take your advice... or not.

> **Example**
>
> You need to find a warm place to leave the plants. This could be:
> * a conservatory
> * an airing cupboard
> * on a high shelf

My parents call it advising — I call it nagging...

State what you're going to advise on, reassure the reader and then give them an action plan. With these three little steps you too can fulfil your life's ambition and become an agony aunt.

Writing a Speech

Speeches need to be interesting and informative. They are written to persuade an audience.

Speeches are Written to be Spoken

1) It's really important to remember that what you're writing is intended to be <u>said aloud</u>.

2) This means it doesn't need to be as <u>formal</u> as some other writing tasks.

3) You do need to use correct <u>grammar</u>, though.

4) Try to <u>impress</u> your audience with a range of vocabulary that will grab their <u>attention</u>.

5) Writing the speech in advance gives you the chance to be <u>prepared</u>, so <u>show off</u> a bit!

Make your writing Memorable

It's essential that your speech <u>stands out</u>. There are loads of things
you can do to make sure your speech comes alive...

- Use <u>interesting similes and metaphors</u>.

- Add in some <u>rhetorical questions</u> to get the audience's attention.
  These are questions that <u>don't</u> expect a <u>response</u>, and they can make
  the audience <u>think</u> about your points and <u>engage</u> with them.

- Using <u>repetition</u> is a good way of <u>reinforcing</u> your points.

- <u>Lists of three</u> are really <u>persuasive</u> devices. They make you sound <u>certain</u>,
  e.g. 'You should buy this house because it is available, attractive <u>and</u> affordable."

Think about Purpose and Audience

The point of a speech is to <u>persuade</u>. It needs to be <u>striking</u> but also easy to
<u>understand</u>. Use <u>emotive language</u> to write a <u>powerful</u> and <u>engaging</u> speech.
Using "I" and "you" will also help you appeal <u>directly</u> to your audience.

Emotive language is language that has an emotional effect on the reader.

Don't bore your audience with too much jargon or slang.

From the beginning of this fiscal year, this company has adopted a belt-and-braces approach to market capitalisation, dictated by a 3% dip in share-price...

There's too much jargon in this speech...

Ladies and gentlemen, have you ever wondered why hip-hop music is so popular? I love hip-hop because of its groovy beat, its rhythmic feel and its iconic artists...

...but this one is a lot easier to understand, so it's more engaging.

I think I've lost the power of speech...

Yep, this page is just that amazing. Remember — speeches should be as powerful as possible.
Use the tips on this page to help you write a stimulating, persuasive and engaging speech.

Section Six — Types of Writing

Writing About Texts That You Have Read

Here's some general advice for answering questions on your own reading...

Think of the **Texts** you've **Read**

1) Some writing questions will ask you to write about <u>texts you've read</u>.

2) The question will often ask you to give a <u>personal response</u> about something you've read, so be sure to give your <u>opinion</u>.

3) You should treat these questions like any other — <u>underline the key words</u> and make a <u>plan</u> based on what the question is asking you to do.

4) Think about the texts you've read and <u>decide</u> which ones you could use to write an <u>interesting</u> and <u>relevant</u> answer.

5) Think about the <u>effect</u> the text(s) had on you and how the <u>author achieves this</u>.

> **Q** Have you ever read a text that completely changed your opinion on a major issue? Write about this text, explaining how it achieved this.

If the question asks you to write about 'a text', make sure you only write about <u>one</u>.

> **Q** A conclusive ending always makes for a better reading experience. To what extent have you found this to be true in your own reading?

Using '<u>your own reading</u>' means you can write about <u>more than one text</u>. Try to make some <u>comparisons</u> (see p.45) and use them to say what kind of writing you <u>prefer</u>.

Write a **Personal** response

Have a look at this example. Remember — a '<u>text</u>' or a '<u>book</u>' can be <u>any kind</u> of writing — it doesn't have to be a novel.

> **Q** Write about an introduction to a text that you found particularly effective.

Start with the <u>author</u> and <u>title</u> of the book you have chosen.

Try to remember as much <u>detail</u> from the text as possible.

— Example —

The introduction to Charles Dickens' "Bleak House" had a really strong effect on me and made me want to read the rest of the book. Dickens sets the scene brilliantly and uses a lot of imagery to depict a dreary November morning in gloomy London. I particularly liked the idea of a Megalosaurus waddling around. The way Dickens writes about the fog pressing in from all sides made me feel as if I were in the street...

Your answer can be about <u>anything</u> you've read — it doesn't have to be something you read at school.

Give lots of <u>opinions</u> and try to make your answer really <u>personal</u>.

And how did that make you feel...?

Make sure you give detailed and personal answers to these questions. Use the tips on this page to show what a massive effect this text had on you. Try to sound as enthusiastic as possible.

Writing About Multiple Texts

Looking at multiple texts side by side helps you spot the different styles and techniques writers use.

Look for **Similarities** and **Differences**

1) Writing about multiple texts means <u>comparing two or more texts</u> and looking to see how they're <u>different</u> and how they're <u>similar</u>.

2) Sometimes you'll have to write about texts that seem very <u>different</u>, for example, a <u>poem</u> and an extract from a <u>story</u>.

Don't write about each text **Separately**

1) When you're comparing texts, <u>don't</u> write about <u>one text at a time</u>. Write about them at the <u>same</u> time, making <u>links</u> between them.

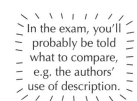
In the exam, you'll probably be told what to compare, e.g. the authors' use of description.

2) For example, you could say how the <u>language</u> in the texts is <u>similar</u>, or <u>different</u>, and give some <u>examples</u>.

3) Here are some things you could look at when you <u>compare</u> texts:

- audience
- purpose
- layout
- mood
- setting
- language
- structure
- perspective

4) So, a <u>plan</u> for a <u>comparing question</u> could look a bit like this:

— Example —

<u>Structure</u>	text 1 is a poem about a terrifying experience in a graveyard text 2 is a story about a zombie apocalypse.
<u>Language</u>	text 1 has lots of adjectives for description, e.g. "ghoulish" text 2 uses metaphors — "the town was a bare wasteland"
<u>Mood</u>	text 1 uses ellipses to create suspense text 2 uses short sentences to create suspense

5) Always try to give an <u>opinion</u>, and don't forget to give <u>evidence</u> to <u>back up</u> your points:

— Example —

Both authors use stylistic techniques to create suspense, but they do it in different ways. In text 1, the author uses ellipses:
      "I couldn't believe what I was seeing..."
However, I think the author of text 2 builds suspense more effectively; he uses a series of short sentences:
      "It was pitch black. Sam could see nothing. He waited."

I was always told not to compare myself to others...

There are loads of things you could mention when comparing texts, and you might not have time to write about all of them. Pick the things that stand out the most, and focus on those.

Writing from Your Point of View

Writing from your own viewpoint can be a bit tricky, but this advice will help you get going.

It could be a *Memory* or *Personal Opinion*

Think about <u>who</u> you're writing for and the <u>purpose</u> of the piece you are writing.
If you can write in any <u>form</u>, think about what's best for <u>getting your feelings across</u>.

(1) Think about the specific <u>details</u> or <u>events</u> that have led you to have a particular opinion.

(2) Include lots of personal <u>anecdotes</u> — you can make them up if you have to, but it's easier if you've got some real ones you can relate to.

(3) Don't be shy about expressing <u>strong emotions</u> like fear or pain — it'll make your piece a lot more <u>powerful</u>.

(4) Don't just say how things look. Think about how things <u>sound</u>, <u>smell</u>, <u>feel</u> and <u>taste</u>.

Have a look at these *Example Tasks*

Some writing tasks, like <u>informal letters</u> and <u>speeches</u>, will naturally involve <u>personal feelings</u>.

Here are a couple of possible question types:

Q Think of a funny moment from your childhood. Write about it in an entertaining way.

Direct spoken <u>question</u> grabs the audience's attention.

A <u>dramatic description</u> sets the scene — remember to use other senses too.

Example

"Where's Dad gone?" asked my brother, looking back to where Dad should have been. We were on our annual walk to Glenbiggle Castle, through the marshy fields to the majestic, imposing, grey stone ruins. If I'm honest, I never usually enjoyed the walk, but this year was different — Dad had slipped over, and reappeared covered from head-to-toe in thick brown mud...

Using specific <u>details</u> makes the text more personal.

<u>Confiding</u> in the reader will help them engage with the story.

Q Write about what, in your experience, makes a good friend.

A <u>chatty</u>, <u>first-person style</u> is perfect for the <u>purpose</u> and <u>audience</u> of this article.

Example

I couldn't believe that Richard had made such a sacrifice for me. We'd only known each other for three months, but if it hadn't been for Rick's selfless quick-thinking, I dread to think what might have happened to the rest of...

Use <u>snappy phrases</u> to get a lot of information into a few words.

I've got a photographic memory...

I just haven't had it developed yet... Whether you're writing about a memory or an opinion, remember the points in the blue boxes. Use all your senses to write a really interesting answer.

Summary Questions

Hoorah, you've nearly completed the section on writing features. Only one final hurdle before you can make your escape — the tiny matter of a few Summary Questions. Make sure you can answer all of these before you move on. If you get some wrong, go back* and check you understand everything. Then try the questions again. Once you can whizz through them without batting an eyelid, it's time to take a well-deserved break.

1) Why is it a good idea to look at your topic from the opposite point of view when you are arguing or persuading?

2) Which of these would be the best sentence to include in an argument against fox hunting?
   a) Fox hunting is responsible for the deaths of a few foxes every year.
   b) Every year, fox hunting results in the violent murder of thousands of innocent foxes.
   c) Last year, fox hunters used three-headed spiders to kill over eighteen billion foxes.

3) Name the five main things that explanations should tell the audience.

4) Informative writing is usually made up of super-long sentences with loads of opinion and exaggeration. True or false?

5) I am writing a leaflet telling people how best to look after their pet camel. Am I writing to:
   a) inform   b) persuade   c) argue?

6) A new sports centre has just opened in your town. Write an article for a local magazine which informs residents about the centre and what's on offer there.

7) Mrs Sue Perior wants to write a letter to her friend, advising her about how to deal with money troubles. What sort of tone should she use to show she understands?

8) If you're writing to advise you should:
   a) tell the person you feel really sorry for them and you don't know how to help,
   b) tell the person exactly what to do and threaten to harass them if they don't, or
   c) give the person a range of possible courses of action and let them choose which one they prefer.

9) Which of these devices will help to make your speech memorable?
   a) exciting similes and metaphors
   b) technical jargon
   c) long, unstructured ramblings about your feelings on the subject
   d) rhetorical questions
   e) repetition

10) Think about the advantages and disadvantages of students bringing mobile phones to school. Have a go at writing a speech in which you argue for one side rather than the other.

11) If you need to answer a question about your own reading, you should:
    a) pick your favourite book and write a long explanation of why you think it's amazing,
    b) write a bullet-point list of all the books you've ever read, or
    c) choose a book that you've read that is relevant to the question.

12) Give four things that you could write about when you're comparing texts.

13) List three things you should do when you're writing about a memory or personal opinion.

* You won't find the answers to questions 6 and 10 in the section because they require
  a personal response — but planning and writing them is useful practice for your exams.

Use Different Words

A good way to make your writing more interesting is to use lots of different words.

Use **Different Words** for the **Same Thing**

English has lots of words that mean the <u>same thing</u> as other words. That sounds a bit pointless. But it's actually <u>really handy</u>. Writing is very <u>dull</u> if it uses the same words all the time.

Have a look at these two pieces of writing and you'll see what I mean.

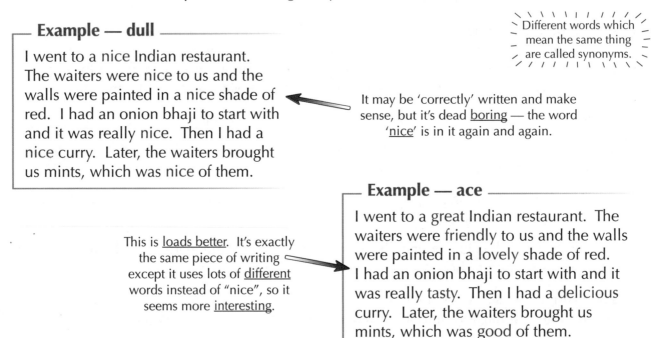

> Different words which mean the same thing are called synonyms.

┌─ Example — dull ─────

I went to a nice Indian restaurant. The waiters were nice to us and the walls were painted in a nice shade of red. I had an onion bhaji to start with and it was really nice. Then I had a nice curry. Later, the waiters brought us mints, which was nice of them.

It may be 'correctly' written and make sense, but it's dead <u>boring</u> — the word '<u>nice</u>' is in it again and again.

┌─ Example — ace ─────

I went to a great Indian restaurant. The waiters were friendly to us and the walls were painted in a lovely shade of red. I had an onion bhaji to start with and it was really tasty. Then I had a delicious curry. Later, the waiters brought us mints, which was good of them.

This is <u>loads better</u>. It's exactly the same piece of writing except it uses lots of <u>different</u> words instead of "nice", so it seems more <u>interesting</u>.

It's easy to fall into the trap of using the same word all the time — especially <u>adjectives</u> like "<u>nice</u>" or "<u>weird</u>". You've got to keep an eye out and make sure you don't do it.

Look out for **Verbs** as well as **Adjectives**

There are oodles of <u>different</u> verbs too.

Look at this little piece of writing. It becomes a lot more interesting just by adding two <u>new verbs</u> instead of repeating "ran" three times.

I ran to the post box with a letter, then I ran to the shop for some chocolate. After that I ran home so I wasn't late for tea.

I ran to the post box with a letter, then I hurried to the shop for some chocolate. After that I raced home so I wasn't late for tea.

e.g.
You could say Jump
or Leap   or Bound

Use <u>different</u> words whenever you can — they make your writing <u>tons better</u>.

Clever words really **Stand Out**

Using <u>different</u> words is a good start.
If you can use <u>different and clever</u> words, you're laughing teacakes.

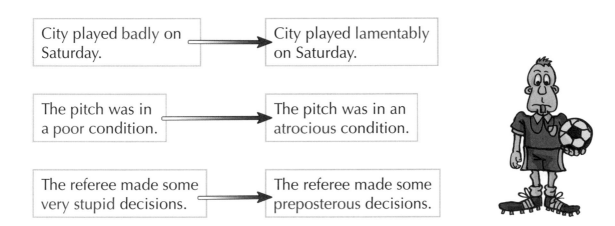

City played badly on Saturday.	→	City played lamentably on Saturday.
The pitch was in a poor condition.	→	The pitch was in an atrocious condition.
The referee made some very stupid decisions.	→	The referee made some preposterous decisions.

You can't use long fancy words <u>all</u> the time — that'd just sound <u>daft</u>.
But you'll get better marks if you throw them in <u>now and then</u>.
So remember this rule:

> Every <u>now and then</u>, try to replace a <u>short</u>
> and <u>simple</u> word with a <u>long</u> and <u>clever</u> one.

Of course, you have to know some <u>clever words</u> before you can use them. Get into the habit
of <u>looking up</u> words you don't know in the <u>dictionary</u>. You really can't know too many words.

Use a **Dictionary** to help you **Develop** your **Vocabulary**

1) Spelling is <u>really important</u>. Using a clever word is like doing a trick
   on a skateboard — it's only really impressive if you get it right.

2) If you're not sure how to spell a word, check it in the dictionary.
   Then try to <u>learn</u> the spelling for the next time you need it.

3) And one last thing — <u>DON'T</u> use a long word if you're <u>not sure</u> what it means.

Use long words? — OK, wooooorrdddsssssss...

You'll get much better marks if you make your writing interesting. The first step is to use different
words, then throw in some long and clever ones and hey presto — it'll be fascinating.

Don't Be Boring

Here are a couple more tricks that'll help you make your writing more interesting.

Don't use "And" and "Then" too much

This is something loads of people do, but it makes your writing a great big <u>yawn</u>.

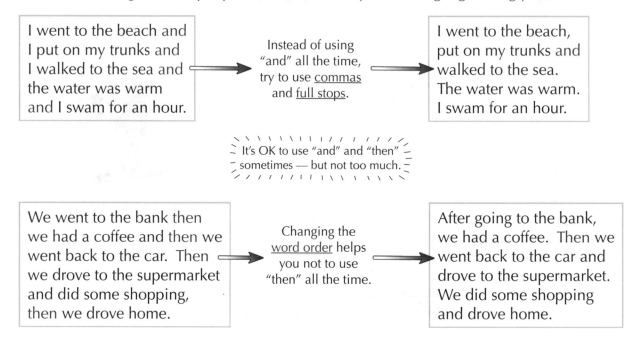

I went to the beach and I put on my trunks and I walked to the sea and the water was warm and I swam for an hour.

Instead of using "and" all the time, try to use <u>commas</u> and <u>full stops</u>.

I went to the beach, put on my trunks and walked to the sea. The water was warm. I swam for an hour.

It's OK to use "and" and "then" sometimes — but not too much.

We went to the bank then we had a coffee and then we went back to the car. Then we drove to the supermarket and did some shopping, then we drove home.

Changing the <u>word order</u> helps you not to use "then" all the time.

After going to the bank, we had a coffee. Then we went back to the car and drove to the supermarket. We did some shopping and drove home.

Don't start all your sentences the Same Way

This is another thing that makes your writing <u>dull</u> and <u>boring</u>.

There was a chill in the air as Jo walked towards the house. There was nobody around. There was a big oak door and Jo knocked on it. There was a scream from inside the house.

This says the same things, but in a <u>more interesting</u> way...

There was a chill in the air as Jo walked towards the house. Nobody was around. Jo knocked on the big oak door. A scream came from inside.

Think of <u>different</u> ways to <u>start</u> your sentences.
It isn't that hard, and it makes your writing much more <u>interesting</u> to read.

Use a **Variety** of **Short** and **Long** sentences

Sometimes a short sentence works best and sometimes a long one does. Neither of them work well all of the time. It's best to use a variety of different lengths.

— **Example** —

I needed to catch a train which left at one o'clock and I checked my watch and I was late so I decided to run, but the streets were busy and I kept having to dodge people. Finally I crossed the road and got to the station where I saw the train hadn't left, so I looked at my watch again and it was fast.

The first example uses all long sentences, and the second example uses all short sentences. They're both as dull as dishwater because there's no variety.

— **Example** —

I needed to catch a train. It left at one o'clock. I checked my watch. I was late. I decided to run. The streets were busy. I kept having to dodge people. It seemed to take ages. Finally I got to the station. The train hadn't left. I looked at my watch again. It was fast.

But with some long and some short sentences, this passage is loads more interesting.

— **Example** —

I was walking to the station. I needed to catch a train which left at one o'clock. I checked my watch and I was late so I decided to run, but the streets were busy and I kept having to dodge people, which slowed me down. Finally I crossed the road and got to the station, where I saw the train hadn't left. I looked at my watch again. It was fast.

Don't use too many **Clichés** — they get **Boring**

1) Some figures of speech are used so often that they become boring — they're called clichés.

2) You hear them a lot when people are talking about sport.

| The atmosphere is electric. | I'm as sick as a parrot. | It isn't over until the fat lady sings. |

3) You can get away with using some clichés in your writing, but don't use too many — people will think you haven't got anything original to say.

Hunting wild pigs — nope, that'd be 'boaring'...

These things make your writing boring: using "and" and "then" too much, starting your sentences the same way, and using all long sentences or all short sentences. Just don't do it.

Adjectives

Adjectives are great for making your writing more interesting.

Describe things with Adjectives

1) <u>Adjectives</u> are describing <u>words</u>.

2) They're a quick and easy way to <u>spice up</u> your writing.

Just <u>one</u> little adjective can completely change the <u>impression</u> you get from a sentence.

| I ate a meal. | I ate a delicious meal. | I ate a disgusting meal. |

And with <u>three</u> or <u>four</u> adjectives, you can really start to build up a picture.

| I ate a delicious, sumptuous, lovingly prepared meal. | I ate a disgusting, rancid, undercooked meal. |

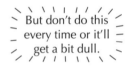

But don't do this every time or it'll get a bit dull.

Adjectives give you a Picture

Have a look at this piece of writing. It's the <u>adjectives</u> that really tell you what this <u>place is like</u>. <u>Without</u> them you <u>wouldn't</u> get much of an <u>idea</u> at all.

Jordios is a quiet, sleepy village on the remote island of Toonos, 40 miles from Athens. Miles of unspoilt, sandy beaches stretch along the deserted coastline. The air is thick with the sweet smell of tall, elegant pine trees.

Rickety wooden fishing boats set off every morning from the small, picturesque harbour. In the evenings the locals gather in the cosy, welcoming tavernas for a friendly chat over a refreshing drink, and a game of table football.

Jug Suppliers — they give you pitchers...

Adjectives are a great way of describing things effectively. Putting them in your writing is like using herbs and spices when you're cooking. They make everything a bit more tasty.

Section Seven — Using Language Effectively

Comparisons

Another good way to describe something is to compare it to something else.

Less than, *More* than, the *Least*, the *Most*...

1) <u>Comparisons</u> are a great way to build up a <u>picture</u> of something.

2) They sound <u>interesting</u> and they create a big <u>effect</u> in your reader's mind.

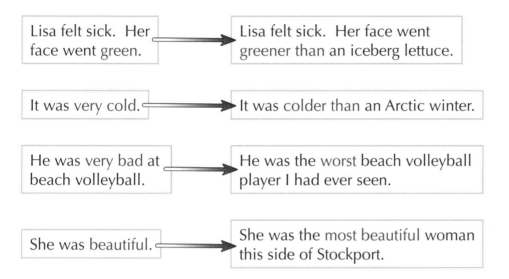

Lisa felt sick. Her face went green.	Lisa felt sick. Her face went greener than an iceberg lettuce.
It was very cold.	It was colder than an Arctic winter.
He was very bad at beach volleyball.	He was the worst beach volleyball player I had ever seen.
She was beautiful.	She was the most beautiful woman this side of Stockport.

3) The key to making a good comparison is to pick something <u>sensible</u>. It's no good saying "it was colder than a pair of scissors", or "Lisa's face went as green as a doorbell".

Careful — don't write "More Better"

When you're making a comparison, you must <u>EITHER</u> say "more... than" or "the most...". <u>Alternatively</u>, with some words, you can use the form of the word that ends in "er" or "est". <u>DON'T EVER DO BOTH</u>.

You are more intelligent than a brick.

NOT "more intelligenter". ⟸ "Intelligenter" isn't a word.
Use a <u>dictionary</u> if you're
unsure of a word.

You are the most sporty person I know.

NOT "most sportiest".

Ted is the cleverest boy in school.

NOT the "most cleverest".

Suzanne is prettier than her sister.

NOT "more prettier".

This rented house is the smallest — it's 'leased'...

Comparisons are another top way of making your writing more interesting — they're the greatest. But don't get confused — you can use more/most, or you can use the er/est ending. Not both.

Summary Questions

So now you know loads of tricks to help you make your writing interesting. Now you just need to learn it all and remember to use it. Interesting writing isn't something you can do just like that — you have to practise it so it becomes natural. The next time you write a letter, a postcard or even a shopping list, have a go at popping in just a little of the fancy stuff — an inexpensive pumpkin, a lemon as sour as my sister, a bottle of chilli sauce as hot as the sun...

1) For each of the sentences below, change the underlined word to make it more interesting.
   a) The cake was <u>nice</u>.   b) Our holiday was <u>great</u>.   c) That was a <u>rubbish</u> film.

2) List three other verbs that could be used to replace 'to say'.

3) How often should you aim to use long and clever words?

4) What can you do to avoid using the word 'and' too much?

5) Rewrite the paragraph below to make it more interesting.
   When Olav arrived, we ate some food then we watched a film and then we played a game. When Helga arrived, the three of us went to the park then we had ice creams and then we went home.

6) Why is it a bad idea to start all your sentences the same way?

7) Is it a good idea to make all of your sentences long and complex? Why / why not?

8) When is it OK to use clichés?
   a) Now and again.
   b) Most of the time.
   c) As frequently as you can.

9) Add adjectives to each of the sentences below to make them more descriptive.
   a) Joseph and Heather walked along the path to the sea.
   b) The car sped through the forest, passing the cottage.
   c) The cow crept into the room, careful not to touch the vase.
   d) There was a noise when the parrot approached the tree.
   e) The man didn't know what was under the table.

10) Which of these are wrong?
   a) You're weirder than me.
   b) She's my bestest friend.
   c) He's more insane, though.
   d) I'm the most funniest.
   e) We're the most charming.
   f) They're much more better.
   g) Jo is intelligenter than Dani.

Introduction to the CASE Paper

The CASE Paper is a bit different from Common Entrance — you'll be told if you're entered for it.

You might sit a **CASE** paper

1) CASE stands for <u>C</u>ommon <u>A</u>cademic <u>S</u>cholarship <u>E</u>xamination.

2) This paper is a bit <u>different</u> from the Common Entrance exam (see p.1). You only have to answer <u>three questions</u>, but they require <u>longer</u>, <u>more developed</u> answers.

3) There's the opportunity to pick up some <u>extra marks</u>, if you write your answers using accurate <u>spelling</u>, <u>punctuation</u> and <u>grammar</u>.

There are **Three Questions** worth **30 Marks** each

1) The CASE Paper lasts <u>1 hour 45 minutes</u>.

2) In that time, you'll have to answer <u>three questions</u>.

3) That means you'll have just over <u>half an hour</u> to answer each question, with a bit of time left at the end to <u>check your work</u>.

4) The paper is worth <u>100 marks</u> — that's <u>30 marks</u> for each of the <u>questions</u>, plus <u>10 extra marks</u> for excellent <u>spelling</u>, <u>punctuation</u>, <u>grammar</u> and <u>expression</u>.

There are **Two Reading** questions...

1) The reading questions involve some <u>literary passages</u> (they could be <u>poems</u> or <u>prose</u>) that have a <u>common theme</u>, e.g. love, family, or the countryside.

2) There'll be <u>one</u> reading question <u>per</u> text.

3) The reading questions usually ask you to write a <u>commentary</u> on the text — see <u>p.56</u> for more about writing commentaries.

...and **One Writing** question

1) For the writing section, you'll have a <u>choice</u> of <u>two questions</u>.

2) One question will normally ask you to <u>compare and contrast</u> the two texts you've already read for the reading questions.

See p.58 for more information on the writing question.

3) The other question will usually give you the opportunity to write an <u>imaginative</u> piece of <u>prose</u> based on a <u>theme</u> related to the reading passages.

Read this page again — just in CASE...

The CASE paper is pretty different from the Common Entrance 13+ English exams, so if you are going to be doing it, it's worth taking a bit of time to get your head around the structure of it.

The Reading Questions

'The Reading Questions' — worst name for a band ever...

You might be asked to write a *Commentary*

1) A <u>commentary</u> is an <u>essay</u> where you pick out <u>features</u> from a text to <u>comment</u> on.

2) Make sure you <u>read the question carefully</u> — it will give you something to <u>focus</u> on, e.g. how a <u>setting</u> is used, or what you think about a certain <u>character</u>.

3) Some questions contain bits of <u>information</u> about the <u>text</u> or its <u>author</u> — think about how you might be able to <u>use</u> this information in your <u>answer</u>.

> **Q** Text A is a poem by William Blake, who was a famous poet and painter. Write a detailed commentary explaining how the poem captivates the reader. **[30]**

This question is asking you to think about <u>how</u> the poem <u>captivates</u> the reader — you'd need to think about the <u>effect</u> that the poem has on the reader, and the <u>ways</u> in which the poet achieves this.

The question tells you that Blake was also a <u>famous painter</u> — you could use this in your answer, e.g. "Blake's ability as a painter helps him to create vivid pictures in the reader's mind."

4) Don't be afraid to give your own <u>opinions</u> in your answer — just make sure that you <u>back them up</u> with evidence from the <u>text</u> (see p.22-26).

5) If you <u>disagree</u> with a statement made in the question, then <u>say so</u>. The examiner wants you to show that you've got your <u>own</u> opinion, and that you can <u>back it up</u> successfully.

You need to *Infer* what's going on in the text

1) "<u>Inferring</u>" means drawing a sensible conclusion about <u>what something means</u> or <u>why something has been used</u>, based on your <u>reading</u> of the text.

> Jack's face turned as red as a beetroot. He clenched his fists and exhaled noisily.

You could <u>infer</u> from this extract that Jack is <u>angry</u>. The text <u>doesn't actually say</u> that he's angry, but it's the <u>most logical conclusion</u>.

2) When you infer something, you should always <u>back it up</u> with an <u>example</u> or <u>evidence</u> from the <u>text</u>. Here are some things to <u>look out</u> for:

figurative language (p.14-15)	sentence structure (p.50-51)	irony and symbolism (p.18)	poetic techniques (p.19-20)

3) When you <u>spot something</u> in the text, ask yourself — "<u>why</u> has the author used it?" and "<u>what effect</u> does it have on the <u>reader</u>?".

4) You need to <u>read between the lines</u> to see if there is a <u>hidden meaning</u> behind a word or phrase. Authors often use <u>irony</u> or <u>symbolism</u> to give their texts an <u>extra layer</u> of <u>meaning</u>.

A *Good Plan* is key to a *Good Answer*

1) Once you've got some ideas to write about, you need to scribble down a <u>plan</u> with your <u>main points</u>.

2) The plan <u>isn't marked</u>, so you don't need to worry about writing in full sentences — it's for you to <u>refer</u> to whilst you're writing.

3) It's a good idea to <u>note down</u> any <u>quotations</u> (and their <u>line numbers</u>) — this will be a good <u>reminder</u> and will help you to <u>find them quickly</u> when you're ready to write about them.

4) Don't forget to plan your <u>introduction</u> and <u>conclusion</u> — making a <u>link</u> to your introduction is a good way to <u>conclude</u> your commentary.

A *Good Structure* helps your answer to *Flow*

1) A good <u>structure</u> means that your ideas are <u>presented clearly</u> and in a <u>logical order</u>.

2) Thinking about a rough structure will help you make sure you <u>include</u> all of your <u>key points</u>.

3) You need to consider how your answer will <u>flow</u> — it should move <u>smoothly</u> from one point to the next. See <u>p.61</u> for some ideas on <u>linking paragraphs</u>.

4) Here are <u>two possible ways</u> you could structure an answer to the question from p.56:

> **Q** Text A is a poem by William Blake, who was a famous poet and painter. Write a detailed commentary explaining how the poem captivates the reader. [30]

Work in a logical order

<u>Opening</u>: dramatic opening with repetition and alliteration — grabs attention.

<u>Middle</u>: lots of rhetorical questions and rhyming couplets — keeps attention.

<u>Ending</u>: the opening stanza is repeated, but with one change — reader taken by surprise.

This approach <u>automatically</u> gives your answer structure, as you're following the <u>structure</u> of the text.

Work through the features

<u>Rhyme</u>: follows a pattern, lots of rhyming couplets — keeps interest as reader anticipates next line ending.

<u>Rhetorical questions</u>: used in a similar way to rhyme — the reader wonders if there are any answers.

<u>Repetition</u>: repetition of these rhetorical questions emphasises the poem's central theme.

This approach is a bit <u>trickier</u>, but if you <u>link</u> your <u>paragraphs</u> well, it can be successful.

Scone, cream, jam, scone — my favourite structure...

It's tempting in the exam to start writing as soon as you've thought of some good ideas, but putting them into a plan, with a structure, will help create a logical answer which flows beautifully.

The Writing Questions

For the writing section of the paper, you have a choice to make...

*You can **Choose** to **Compare** the **Reading Texts**...*

1) The <u>comparison</u> question will ask you to <u>compare</u> and <u>contrast</u> the two texts you've read in the <u>reading section</u>.

2) You'll be given something <u>specific</u> to <u>focus on</u>, e.g. the writers' use of emotions or the way that tension is developed in the passages.

> **Q** Compare and contrast Blake's and Kipling's descriptions of tigers. [30]

— Example —

<u>Imagery</u>: both authors focus on the tigers' eyes — Blake mentions "fire"; Kipling uses "blazing" — both have a fierce intensity.

<u>Verbs</u>: Kipling's tiger seems frantic — lots of active verbs are used. However, the tiger in Blake's poem doesn't actually move — verbs are a lot less active.

<u>Symbolism</u>: fire is used to symbolise Blake's tiger, thunder to describe Kipling's — both show danger and a sense of strength.

The question is asking you to look at the <u>descriptions</u>, so you'll need to think about the different <u>techniques</u> the authors have used.

Make sure that you write about <u>both texts</u> at the <u>same time</u>. See <u>p.45</u> for more on this.

*...or do some **Creative Writing***

Make sure you <u>think outside the box</u> to get bucket-loads of marks for your creative writing:

1) <u>Avoid</u> writing something that sounds like a <u>cliché</u> (see p.51) — steer clear of vampire love-stories. Think of the most <u>logical</u> thing to write about, and do something <u>completely different</u>.

2) Use lots of <u>impressive vocabulary</u> (see p.48-49).

3) Stick in some <u>figurative language</u>, like similes and metaphors (p.14-15).

4) <u>Vary the length</u> of your <u>sentences</u>. Don't be afraid to use <u>unusual word order</u> — you <u>don't</u> have to follow <u>all</u> of the <u>rules</u> with creative writing.

Don't just stick these techniques in all over the place, though — make sure they fit your text.

> **Q** Write an imaginative story or poem, entitled *Scared*. [30]

— Example —

Don't write about a haunted house or graveyard — this story <u>avoids</u> sounding like a <u>cliché</u> by being set in a <u>supermarket</u>.

Martha crept forwards, with the bright, white lights illuminating her hunched body. One step. Then another. Her trolley creaked as she edged it onwards, groaning under the weight of tins, bags and vegetables. Martha's heart was racing faster and faster, and the time to face up to her fear was approaching with an even greater speed...

In a piece of creative writing, you <u>don't</u> always have to use <u>full sentences</u>.

Try to use some <u>figurative language</u>, e.g. personification.

C-r-e-a-t-i-v-e---W-r-i-t-i-n-g---i-s---f-u-n...

Maybe don't be that creative, though — this is an exam we're talking about. Use lots of great vocabulary and figurative language if you do the creative writing option, but don't go too crazy.

Paragraphs

Paragraphs are a pain, but your writing is clearer when you use 'em. You know it makes sense.

Always use Paragraphs

It's not enough to use paragraphs <u>some</u> of the time — you need to use them <u>all</u> the time — in <u>stories</u>, <u>essays</u>, <u>letters</u>... in <u>ANYTHING</u> and <u>EVERYTHING</u> you write.

Paragraphs make things Clear

A paragraph is a <u>group</u> of <u>sentences</u>. These sentences talk about the <u>same thing</u>, or <u>follow on</u> from each other.

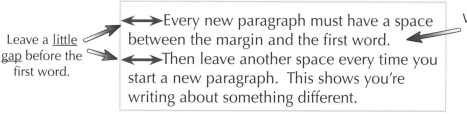

Leave a <u>little</u> <u>gap</u> before the first word.

Every new paragraph must have a space between the margin and the first word.
Then leave another space every time you start a new paragraph. This shows you're writing about something different.

When you finish the <u>last line</u> of the paragraph, <u>just stop</u>.

Start a New Paragraph for Each Point in an essay

Paragraphs help make your essay <u>clearer</u>.
A new paragraph shows that you're writing about <u>something new</u>.

— **Example** —————————————

This is a <u>new</u> <u>point</u>, so start a new paragraph.

 The idea that school uniforms hide differences between the rich and poor is false. Everyone can tell whose uniform came from a discount shop and whose is designer.
 Supporters of school uniform say that they don't want to turn school into a "fashion parade". In fact, this is exactly what they are doing when they point out the tiny ways in which a skirt or jumper doesn't quite fit the rules.

Para-, para- paragraphs — oh, oh, oh, oh, oh, oh-oh oh...

Paragraphs — love 'em (phwoooar) or hate 'em (bleuuurgh), you've got to use 'em. Start a new paragraph every time you start a sentence with a brand new idea, angle or argument.

Using and Linking Paragraphs

You need to know when to start a new paragraph — you can't just guess I'm afraid.

Here's the **Golden Rule** for **Paragraphs**

The Golden Rule — Start a new paragraph every time <u>something changes</u>.

When you talk about a **New Person**

> Tanya looked at the scene in despair. She couldn't believe that eight soldiers could make such a mess. She sighed and started to pick up the biscuits and crisps.
>
> A friendly face popped round the door. It was Brian. He watched Tanya grovelling around in the mess for a second or two before he spoke up.

This paragraph is about <u>Tanya</u>.

This paragraph is about <u>Brian</u>.

When **Someone New** speaks

> "Please don't do that on your own, Tanya," said Brian. "Come on, I'll help you clear up," he offered.
>
> "Thanks, Brian, you're a star," replied Tanya appreciatively. "Where's everyone else? I thought there were five volunteers to clear up."
>
> "They're all dancing over there," he explained.

Someone <u>new</u> is speaking, so you need a <u>new</u> paragraph.

The <u>same</u> person is speaking here, so you <u>don't</u> need a new paragraph.

A new paragraph for a **New Place**...

The shopping mall was deserted. The guards scratched their heads. Where was everybody?

Outside Bernie's gourmet chip shop in the High Street, it was a rather different story. The crowd was pushing and shoving to get to the door. "Give us battered rat!" they cried. "Give us rat on a stick!"

The story has <u>moved</u> to the chip shop, so this is a <u>new paragraph</u>.

...or for a **Different Time**

This is talking about a long time <u>afterwards</u>.

At last it was over. The voice called out again, "Are you all right?" I barely had the strength to answer. I was giddy with relief. Soon I would be out of the cave and home. I don't think about my ordeal that much. When I look back, it seems like something that happened to somebody else.

Make sure you **Link** your **Paragraphs**

Paragraphs need to flow <u>smoothly</u> from one to the other. This keeps your writing <u>organised</u>. You can use <u>words</u> and <u>phrases</u> at the <u>start</u> of your paragraphs to <u>link</u> them together.

Here are a few examples:

Furthermore...   Therefore...   Firstly...   Another view is...

Secondly...   In addition...   Also...   On the other hand...

... that's one of the main reasons why I'd make a good prefect.
Furthermore, I work very hard, especially in a team...

The word '<u>furthermore</u>' shows that this paragraph <u>links</u> to the previous one.

... which shows that Justine is a really evil character.
On the other hand, Justine has every reason to hate Katrina...

The phrase '<u>on the other hand</u>' shows that you're going to look at <u>both sides</u> of the argument.

A herby fish dish — thyme and plaice...

A new point, person, speaker, place or time (phew) means you have to start a new paragraph. And remember to link them together — don't leave them floating around. They get confused.

Staying in the Right Tense

Switching tenses is a big no-no. That means you've got to learn to use tenses properly.

Don't change tenses in your writing by Mistake

Once you've picked a tense, you'll usually need to stick to it.
Make sure all the verbs agree with each other.

This is in the past tense.

Another past verb.

> As Andy tried to hide the money, he heard a siren in the distance. Suddenly, he sees a light.

This one's wrong — it's in the present tense, but it should be in the past tense. The correct form of the verb is 'saw'.

Use Past Verbs in Past Writing

1) Be consistent — don't switch tenses accidentally.
   Stay in one tense so it's clear what's going on.

2) If you start writing in the past, you've got to stay in the past.

> The day I finished reading "Jane Eyre" by Charlotte Brontë was one of the saddest days of my life. I loved the book and had grown to love Jane. I knew I would miss her a lot.

If you're writing about the past you should use the past tense.

All the verbs here are past forms.

Be Especially Careful with the Present

You need the present for some essays, but don't mix past and present forms by mistake.

> Even though Alex is injured, Roy felt he has to pick him for the team.

'felt' is past tense, but the rest of the sentence is in the present.

> Even though Alex is injured, Roy feels he has to pick him for the team.

This is how the sentence should be written — all of the verbs are in the present tense.

Consistency of tenses — a sticky business...

Sticking to the same tense — it sounds so simple. But when you're in a hurry, it's easy to put the wrong one down without thinking. Learn this page and remember your tenses when you write.

Section Nine — Grammar

Subject-Verb Agreement

Learn these key points on subject-verb agreement — they'll help you gain marks in the exam.

Verbs need to *Agree* with their *Subject*

The <u>subject</u> is the person or thing <u>doing</u> the action.

Some <u>verbs</u> change <u>depending</u> on who is <u>doing</u> the action.

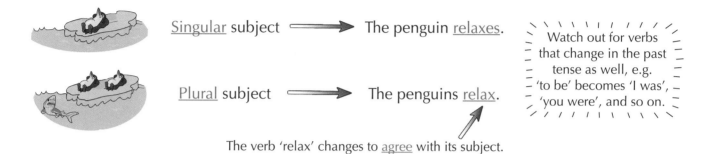

<u>Singular</u> subject ⟹ The penguin <u>relaxes</u>.

<u>Plural</u> subject ⟹ The penguins <u>relax</u>.

Watch out for verbs that change in the past tense as well, e.g. 'to be' becomes 'I was', 'you were', and so on.

The verb 'relax' changes to <u>agree</u> with its subject.

Be **Careful** *with* **Long Sentences**

In <u>long sentences</u>, the <u>verb</u> and the <u>subject</u> can get <u>separated</u> — make sure they still <u>agree</u>.

Animals that are raised in captivity, such as the giraffe, is unlikely to survive once they are released back into the wild.

This sentence doesn't work because the verb isn't right — you can't say "<u>animals is</u> unlikely to survive".

It should be "<u>are</u>".

Make sure you can make **Common Verbs** *agree*

People often use the wrong forms of '<u>to be</u>' and '<u>to have</u>'.
Make sure you learn the <u>correct forms</u>.

to be		
I am	you are	he/she/it is
	we are	they are

to have		
I have	you have	he/she/it has
	we have	they have

A great page — I think you'll agree...

There are loads of weird verb forms out there that you just have to learn. We've mainly covered the <u>present</u> tense here, but don't forget — a lot of verbs have irregular <u>past</u> and <u>future</u> tenses too.

Summary Questions

Well, here we are at the end of another section already, and what d'you know, it's time for a set of Summary Questions. Remember, the point of these little jokers is to make sure that you've learnt something from the last five pages. Go through them, and don't go peeking at the next section until you've got them all right. Ooh, I can be tough when I want to be...

1) What is a paragraph?

2) What should you do at the start of a new paragraph?

3) What effect do paragraphs have on your writing?

4) What is the golden rule for starting a new paragraph?

5) You should start a new paragraph when:
   a) the same person is speaking,
   b) you are writing about a new person,
   c) you are writing about a new place,
   d) you are writing about the same person,
   e) a new person is speaking, or
   f) you are writing about a different time.

6) The following piece is really confusing.
   Turn it into a nice clear bit of writing by re-writing it with three proper paragraphs:

   The biggest challenge facing junior league football today is the sheer number of red and yellow cards issued by referees. There is no doubt that standards of discipline have fallen sharply. This season, 185 yellow cards and 44 red cards have already been issued, with four players facing a four-match ban. Ten years ago, only 53 yellow cards were shown across the whole season, and only eight players were sent off by referees. Players were much better behaved and did not dare to argue with referees. Hector Dalrymple, Chairman of the UK Federation of Under-16 Football Clubs, said last week that the current situation is "reaching crisis point". Some, like Julian Fortescue of Edenhall School, disagree.

7) List five words or phrases that can be used to link paragraphs.

8) Rewrite the sentence below so that both of the verbs are in the same tense.
   "Steven forgot his hockey stick so he borrows one from Mr Mantell."

9) "My older brother Jeremy, like a lot of people, love going to the cinema."
   Why is this sentence wrong?

Basic Punctuation

This stuff is about as basic as grammar gets. People still make mistakes, though, so learn this page.

Remember these Simple Sentence rules...

Right, here are <u>two rules</u> to remember:

① Every sentence <u>starts</u> with a <u>capital letter</u>, and <u>ends</u> with a <u>full stop</u>.

② The names of <u>people</u>, <u>places</u>, <u>organisations</u>, <u>days</u>, <u>months</u> and <u>titles</u> of <u>books</u> and <u>poems</u>
ALL NEED CAPITAL LETTERS.

Here are a couple of examples of the rules in action:

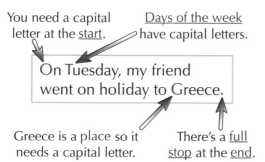

You need a capital letter at the <u>start</u>.

<u>Days of the week</u> have capital letters.

On Tuesday, my friend went on holiday to Greece.

Greece is a place so it needs a capital letter.

There's a <u>full stop</u> at the <u>end</u>.

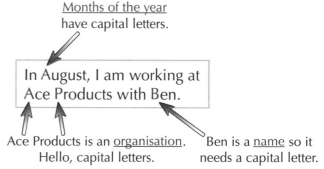

<u>Months of the year</u> have capital letters.

In August, I am working at Ace Products with Ben.

Ace Products is an <u>organisation</u>. Hello, capital letters.

Ben is a <u>name</u> so it needs a capital letter.

Questions need Question Marks

If you're writing a question, make sure you use a <u>question mark</u>.

Boris, can you see Mrs Marple?

Only use One Exclamation Mark

Only ever use <u>one</u> exclamation mark when you're writing a sentence, even if the homework is ridiculously exciting.

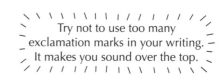
Try not to use too many exclamation marks in your writing. It makes you sound over the top.

<u>One</u> exclamation mark does the job <u>nicely</u>.

It was absolutely amazing! I couldn't believe I was meeting the new pop sensations, No Direction!!!

This makes your writing look like a barcode — and that's just <u>silly</u>.

Getting this wrong — it's a capital crime...

OK, this is something that's so basic you'd only get it wrong if you weren't awake. What you have to do is make sure you can do it in your sleep — that way you won't make any daft mistakes.

Sentences, Phrases and Clauses

It's important that you get to grips with sentences, phrases and clauses...

Every Sentence makes a Clear Point

Make sure that <u>every</u> sentence you write has a <u>clear point</u>.

> *The Golden Rule* — Every sentence must make sense on its own.

A Sentence has to have a Verb

Every sentence you write has to be <u>about</u> something. It can only be <u>about</u> something <u>happening</u> if it's got a <u>verb</u>. (Remember, <u>verbs</u> are <u>doing</u> and <u>being</u> words.)

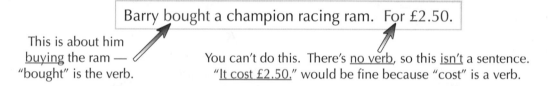

> Barry bought a champion racing ram. For £2.50.

This is about him <u>buying</u> the ram — "bought" is the verb.

You can't do this. There's <u>no verb</u>, so this <u>isn't</u> a sentence. "<u>It cost £2.50.</u>" would be fine because "cost" is a verb.

Use **Phrases** and **Clauses** to **Improve** your **Sentences**

1) <u>Varying</u> the <u>length</u> of your sentences can make your writing <u>more interesting</u>.

2) You can make <u>simple</u> sentences <u>better</u> by joining <u>phrases</u> and <u>clauses</u> together.

- A <u>clause</u> is a part of a sentence which has <u>a subject</u> and <u>a verb</u>.

- A <u>phrase</u> is a part of a sentence which <u>doesn't</u> have <u>a subject</u>, or <u>doesn't</u> have <u>a verb</u> (some phrases might have <u>neither</u>).

3) You can join <u>two clauses</u> together to make a sentence:

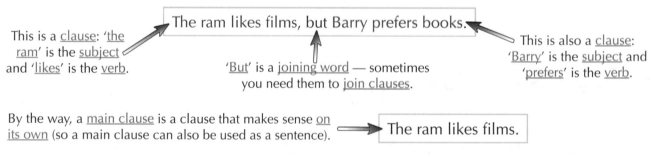

> The ram likes films, but Barry prefers books.

This is a <u>clause</u>: 'the ram' is the <u>subject</u> and '<u>likes</u>' is the <u>verb</u>.

'But' is a <u>joining word</u> — sometimes you need them to <u>join clauses</u>.

This is also a <u>clause</u>: '<u>Barry</u>' is the <u>subject</u> and '<u>prefers</u>' is the <u>verb</u>.

By the way, a <u>main clause</u> is a clause that makes sense <u>on its own</u> (so a main clause can also be used as a sentence).

> The ram likes films.

4) You can also join a <u>clause</u> and a <u>phrase</u> to make a sentence:

> The ram chews Barry's furniture or his slippers.

This is a <u>clause</u> because it has a <u>subject</u> ('<u>the ram</u>') and a <u>verb</u> ('<u>chews</u>').

This is a <u>phrase</u>. It doesn't have a verb. Nothing is happening.

Santa — my favourite type of clause...

This sentence structure stuff may seem pretty easy, but make sure you understand the difference between a phrase, a clause and a main clause — you'll need them again later in this section.

Commas

You'll definitely need some commas in your writing, so make sure you know how to use them.

Use **Commas** to **Break Up** sentences

If your sentence has <u>more than one</u> point, a comma keeps the points <u>separate</u>.
Commas keep the items in <u>lists</u> separate, too.

> I asked him to shut up, but he kept on yelling.

The comma keeps these two bits <u>separate</u>.

Commas add **Extra Bits** to sentences

You can use commas to <u>add extra bits</u> of information into your sentences.

You can add bits to the <u>start</u> and <u>end</u> of sentences...

> After the match, we all went to Kathy's house for tea and toast.

...or to the <u>middle</u> of sentences. The commas go around it like <u>little brackets</u>.

> Annie and Ali, who live next door, have built a new shed.

commas

When you start a sentence with words like "<u>Oh</u>", "<u>Right</u>" or "<u>Well</u>", you need a <u>comma</u> to separate it from the rest of the sentence.

> Oh dear, I think you need to lose that hat.

comma

comma

> Well, I suppose you might just get away with it.

Don't stick them in **All Over** the place

You should <u>only</u> put commas in when you want to <u>break</u> a sentence up into <u>two bits</u>, or when you want to stick in a bit of <u>extra</u> information.

> The Mayor, Mrs Taylor, and the Treasurer, Mr Barker, said today, that the community centre would open on the 14th of August.

<u>This</u> comma's <u>wrong</u> — "said today" and "that the community centre..." go together — they're part of the <u>same</u> bit of info.

Blend in — be a comma chameleon...

Commas keep things apart in sentences. Make sure you use them to bracket off extra bits of information, but don't chuck them around willy-nilly. Learn the right way to use them.

Colons and Semicolons

Colons and semicolons are the big organisers of the punctuation world.

Use *Colons* to *Introduce* a *List*

This is a <u>colon</u>: ⟶ **:**

If you want to <u>introduce</u> a <u>list</u>, you use a colon.

This is what you need to go camping:
one tent, a gas stove, board games,
two saucepans, a kettle and a torch.

<u>Only</u> use a colon to introduce a list if it follows
a <u>main clause</u> (see p.66). If this sentence
started with "you need", you <u>wouldn't</u> use
a colon because that's <u>not</u> a main clause.

A *Colon* can *Introduce* an *Explanation*

Colons are also <u>handy</u> for showing that you're about to <u>explain</u> a point you've just made.

Mr Hackett was feeling very stupid: he'd forgotten to pack any trousers.

Remember, the <u>first part</u> of the
sentence needs to be a <u>main clause</u>
— it has to <u>make sense</u> on its <u>own</u>.

colon

The bit <u>after</u> the colon <u>explains</u> what
was said before — it explains <u>why</u>
Mr Hackett was feeling very stupid.

Use *Semicolons* to *Break Up Lists*

<u>Semicolons</u> can help you to organise <u>long lists</u> and make them <u>easier</u> to <u>read</u>.
They're <u>particularly</u> handy when you want to <u>organise</u> a list that has <u>other punctuation</u> in it too.

The <u>first part</u> of
the sentence is,
you guessed it,
a main clause.

Lizi's reasons for not going to school were quite simple:
she hated being told where to go and when; the school
dinners (which were compulsory) always tasted foul;
and the uniform, a bright yellow, was just not her colour.

The semicolons
divide the list
into <u>sections</u>...

...and then you can
divide these up using
<u>other</u> punctuation.

Semicolons can *Break Up Clauses* in a *Sentence*

You can use semicolons to <u>break</u> up <u>sentences</u>, not just lists.
Both parts of the sentence need to be <u>main clauses</u> and be <u>related</u>.

<u>Both</u> clauses could
be sentences <u>on</u>
<u>their own</u>...

Katie married her childhood friend; her
twin brother, Jacob, married his cat.

...and they're <u>equally</u>
<u>important</u> points.

Colons and semicolons — not just for texting :) ;) ...

Colons and semicolons will make your writing look dead impressive. Remember — colons
introduce things, semicolons break them up. I know which ones I'd rather be friends with...

Section Ten — Punctuation

Apostrophes

Lots of people mess this up — so make sure you know it so well that you'll never forget it.

Use **Apostrophes** to **Show** who **Owns Something**

1) You need to use an apostrophe plus 's' when you're writing about things that <u>belong</u> to people.

| Kulvinder's goldfish have all died. |

The apostrophe shows that the goldfish belong to Kulvinder.

'Men', 'women' and 'children' follow the same rule.

| The women's race was cancelled. |

2) There's an <u>important</u> rule for words <u>ending</u> in '<u>s</u>':

| James's garden is bigger than mine. |

If a <u>single name</u> ends in '<u>s</u>', you <u>still</u> need to add an <u>apostrophe</u> and an '<u>s</u>'...

| I washed the players' kit in soy sauce. |

...but when it's a <u>group</u> of something ending in '<u>s</u>', add an <u>apostrophe</u>, but <u>no 's'</u>.

You can also use **Apostrophes** to **Shorten** words

When you're <u>shortening</u> a <u>word</u> you need to use an <u>apostrophe</u> to show there are <u>missing letters</u>. These are called <u>contractions</u>. Here are some common examples...

I am — I'm	he is — he's	who is — who's
I would — I'd	we are — we're	we will — we'll
I have — I've	they are — they're	does not — doesn't
it is — it's	cannot — can't	will not — won't

See p.74 for more about when to use '<u>it's</u>' with an apostrophe.

'<u>Can't</u>' and '<u>won't</u>' are a bit <u>different</u> — 'can't' is just a shorter version of '<u>cannot</u>', and '<u>won't</u>' <u>doesn't</u> quite <u>match</u> the missing letters from '<u>will not</u>'.

You can use these for <u>informal</u> writing, but for <u>formal</u> stuff, like <u>essays</u>, you should always use the <u>full version</u>.

An award for postmen — a post trophy...

Apostrophes. We just can't ignore the little blighters — remember apostrophes in your writing and where to stick 'em. (I know where I'd like to stick 'em... In a box — never to be seen again.)

Speech Marks

Speech marks do what their name suggests — they show when someone's speaking.

Speech Marks show when someone is Speaking

Every time someone speaks in a sentence you need to shove some speech marks in there.

> "Don't leave the cage door open," warned Sally.

Speech marks surround everything that Sally said.

> Sally warned him not to leave the cage door open.

Careful — this doesn't need speech marks because no one's actually speaking.

Start with a Capital Letter...

Make sure that the spoken bit always starts with a capital letter, even if it isn't at the beginning of your sentence.

> Harry said, "Don't worry, I won't."

It starts with a capital letter.

...Always end with some form of Punctuation

The spoken bits of your sentences need to end with some kind of punctuation. It's usually either a full stop, a comma or a question mark — but make sure you use the right one, and put it inside the speech marks.

> Ruby said, "I knew you shouldn't have trusted Harry."

The sentence is finished, so you need a full stop.

> "He's useless," she declared.

The speech has finished but the sentence hasn't. You need a comma here, not a full stop.

> "Did we feed the bear before it escaped?" asked Jill.

This speech is a question, so it ends with a question mark.

Careful — you don't carry on with a capital letter.

Speech marks — 10 out of 10 for a good 'un...

Don't EVER forget to put speech marks around something that a person's actually saying. The stuff on punctuation in speech marks is a bit harder, so make sure you learn the rules.

Summary Questions

You have to pay attention to all the nitty-gritty things like full stops and apostrophes. It's no good being vaguely aware of punctuation and hoping for the best — you have to know it back to front and inside out. And the only way to make sure you know it all is to go over these questions until you get every single one right — effortlessly.

1) What's wrong with the following sentence?
I've got tickets to see the raiders play the vikings on saturday.

2) How many exclamation marks should you put at the end of a sentence?

3) What's the Golden Rule of Sentences?

4) Re-write this as three proper sentences:
I had to find out where the sound was coming from, as I walked closer I got more and more nervous, I wanted to scream, but nothing came out of my mouth.

5) "Under a palm tree with a cool drink."
Why isn't this a sentence? What's missing from it?

6) Are these proper sentences? If not, write a proper sentence instead:
a) My amazing holiday.   b) The sea was warm.   c) To the beach.

7) What is a) a clause? b) a phrase?

8) Put a comma in the right place to show there are two clear points here:
I tried to warn him but the General still sat down firmly on the broken chair.

9) Put commas in the right places to show which is the extra information:
The Masked Mathematician her hair streaming out behind her hurtled towards the long division sum.

10) Should you use a colon or a semicolon in the following situations:
a) To introduce a list?   b) To break up lists?   c) To break up clauses in a sentence?

11) What two things do apostrophes do?

12) Put an apostrophe into each of the words below to create contractions correctly:
a) cant   b) Id   c) dont   d) whos   e) theyre

13) Put speech marks and correct punctuation into this sentence:
Earth has nothing better than a nice cosy armchair murmured Harry.

14) What's wrong with the following sentence?
Terry said "next week I can show you how the equation was solved"

There/Their/They're and Your/You're

Don't throw away easy marks — learn how to use these commonly confused words correctly.

Learn these **Different** spellings

'There', 'their' and 'they're' <u>sound</u> the same but they have <u>different spellings</u> and <u>meanings</u>:

1) '<u>There</u>' refers to <u>places</u> and <u>positions</u>.

2) '<u>Their</u>' means '<u>belonging to them</u>'.

3) '<u>They're</u>' is short for '<u>they are</u>'.

> There is the dictionary — it's under the table.

> Every reader has their own opinion.

> Sue and Jack were born on the same day. They're having a joint birthday party.

Avoid using *'They're'* in the *Exam*

Try not to use 'they're' in the exam — it's too <u>informal</u>. Make sure you use '<u>they are</u>' instead.

> The first two stanzas include lots of emotional language because they're about the poet's childhood.

→

> The first two stanzas include lots of emotional language because they are about the poet's childhood.

Don't get *'Your'* and *'You're'* Confused

1) '<u>Your</u>' means 'belonging to you'.

> Your spelling and grammar are important in the exam.

This shows that the spelling and grammar <u>belong to you</u>.

2) '<u>You're</u>' is short for 'you are'.

> You're going to have to learn this page if you want to do well.

'<u>You're</u>' is a contraction of "you" and "are".

3) Again, try to <u>avoid</u> using 'you're' in the exam — it's informal. Stick with '<u>you are</u>'.

There, their, they're — it's nearly over...

People always make mistakes with these words. It's easy to do because they sound the same.
This kind of mistake will lose you marks, though, so it's important to get them learnt now.

Weather/Whether and Affect/Effect

These words are a bit tricky. Make sure you don't get your 'a's and 'e's mixed up in the exam.

'Weather' and 'Whether' have different Meanings

'Weather' and 'whether' sound exactly the same. The way they're spelt is also pretty similar, but their uses and meanings are totally different.

Weather

'Weather' is a noun — it refers to the climate.

Whether

'Whether' introduces options.

We're wondering whether you'd like to come sailing with us?

Umm... I'm not sure. Let me check whether the weather is any good or not.

You can leave off 'or not' if you want.

'Affect' and 'Effect' crop up all the time

1) 'Affect' is a verb — it's an action which influences something else.

This potion will affect your life choices.

The potion is doing something to your life choices.

2) 'Effect' is a noun — it's the result of an action.

The potion will have an effect on your life choices.

This is talking about the result of taking the potion.

3) You could invent mnemonics to help you remember these spellings, e.g. to remember that Affect is a Verb and Effect is a Noun:

A mnemonic is a phrase that includes a certain pattern of letters to help you remember something.

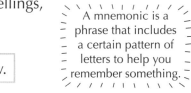
All Vampires Eat Nachos.   or   Ants Vanish Easily Now.

You say effect, I say affect...

Nope, you can't randomly pick a word to use. 'Affect' and 'effect' are separate words — there's a correct one for each situation. The same goes for 'whether' and 'weather'. Learn which is which.

Section Eleven — Spelling

It's/Its and To/Too/Two

These little words are mightily important, so make sure you don't get them wrong in the exam.

'It's' and 'Its' are easily Confused

1) 'It's' is short for 'it is' or 'it has'.

| It's important to feed your cat. |

'It's' is used instead of 'it is'.

| A dog will fetch sticks until it's had enough. |

Here, 'it's' is used instead of 'it has'.

2) 'Its' means belonging to 'it'.

| The fox hurt its tail and jumped into the air. |

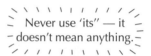
Never use 'its'' — it doesn't mean anything.

3) There's an easy way to check if you've used the right version — replace 'it's' or 'its' with 'it is' or 'it has'. If the sentence makes sense, use 'it's'. If not, use 'its'.

| It is time for lunch now. |

This makes sense, so use 'it's'.

| What happened to it is tail? |

This doesn't work, so use 'its'.

'To', 'Too' and 'Two' mean Different things

'To', 'too' and 'two' have totally different meanings:

1) 'To' can mean 'towards' or it can be part of a verb.

| Eric is going to school. | | I am going to write a brilliant essay. |

2) 'Too' means 'too much' or 'also'.

| Phil ate too much cake. | | Helen baked some scones too. |

3) 'Two' means the number '2'.

| There are only two tortoises at the zoo. |

Is that a to-too train? No, it's an owl — twit two...

You need to get these little words straight in your head. 'Its' is the trickiest because it doesn't use an apostrophe to show possession, which is unusual. All the more reason to get learning...

Where/Were/Wear/We're

These words look similar, but they have different meanings. Make sure you use them correctly.

'Where' is used for Places

The word 'where' is used for <u>places</u> and <u>positions</u>. It can be used as a <u>question word</u> or as part of a sentence.

> Don't forget about the <u>silent 'h'</u> in 'where'. Otherwise it'll say 'were'.

Arrrr, matey. <u>Where</u> are we?

Shiver my timbers, we're back <u>where</u> we started.

'Were' and 'Wear' are Verbs

1) '<u>Were</u>' is the third person plural <u>past</u> form of '<u>to be</u>'.

> When a team finishes bottom of the league, they are relegated.

> When the team finished bottom of the league, they were relegated.

2) You 'wear' <u>clothes</u>.

> You must wear safety goggles when using chemicals.

'We're' is a Shortened Form

'<u>We're</u>' is a contraction of '<u>we are</u>'. You should only use 'we're' in <u>informal</u> situations.

> A contraction is a shortened form of a word (see p.69). The missing letters are marked by an apostrophe.

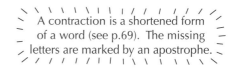

<u>We're</u> very casual and informal, so <u>we're</u> using the shortened form.

<u>We are</u> extremely posh and formal, so <u>we are</u> using the two words separately. None of these ghastly contractions. Perish the thought!

Study this here, there and every-where/were/wear...

These words are seriously important for the exam — they're easy to get wrong because it only takes one wrong letter or a missed apostrophe to change the meaning of a word.

Two Words

Some words might feel like they belong together, but they should be written as two words...

'A lot' means 'many'

'A lot' is another way of saying '<u>many</u>'. It is always written as <u>two words</u>.

> Trevor has written a lot of books.

> The first paragraph contains a lot of similes.

'No one' is two words

You should write 'no one' as <u>two words</u>, not one.

You might also see it written with a hyphen — 'no-one'. This is fine too.

> No one has ever been to Neptune.

> Ian thought that no one had applied for the job.

'Thank you' is also two words

'Thank you' needs to be written as <u>two separate words</u>.

> "Thank you," said the polite parrot.

> It's good to say "thank you" to a shopkeeper.

'All ready' and 'Already' mean different things

1) 'All ready' is a phrase which means '<u>completely prepared</u>'.

> The family is all ready to go on holiday.

> Sara was all ready to take the exam.

2) 'Already' refers to something that has happened <u>before now</u>, or started happening before now.

> I've already bought enough food.

> The sun had already set when Gran woke up.

All ready? All set? All go...

Thank you for getting this far — the section is almost over and you've covered a lot of important spellings. No one is perfect, though, so make sure you've learnt this page properly.

Section Eleven — Spelling

Summary Questions

Ok, so that's the end of the spelling pages. Phew. I am going to have to ask you to complete these questions, though. Go through them now and if there are any that you can't answer, go back and work out what the correct answer should have been. Once you can get all the way through without making any mistakes, you're sorted. You'll be a spelling pro in no time.

1) What's wrong with this sentence? "My parents say their looking for they're lost youth."

2) Why shouldn't you write this sentence in an exam? "The police say they're looking into it."

3) Lisa the Lamb wrote the poem below for her friend. Rewrite the poem, correcting all of the words that are spelt incorrectly.

   Your a ewe like me, you are.
   In fact, your my shining star.
   Of you're friends I think the most of you
   So I'll stick to you're side like glue.

4) Correct this sentence:
   "Do you know weather the whether will be nice for the race tomorrow?"

5) What's the difference between 'affect' and 'effect'? Make up a mnemonic to help you remember the difference between the two.

6) My brother asked me to name two occasions when I would use 'its''.
   Why is this a trick question?

7) How can you check if you've got the right version of 'it's' and 'its'?

8) What is the difference between 'to', 'too' and 'two'?

9) When would you use the word 'where'?

10) What's the difference between 'were' and 'wear'?

11) My aunt is terribly formal — she talks like she's reading an exam script.
    Do you think she would be more likely to use 'we're' or 'we are'?

12) Correct the mistake in the sentence below:
    "My friend and I love the cinema — we go there alot."

13) Which of the words in the brackets should be used to complete the sentence?
    "Samantha drove to the hotel and she was (all ready / already) there when I arrived."

Section Eleven — Spelling

Glossary

adjective	A word that <u>describes</u> a noun, e.g. <u>brown</u> mouse, <u>warm</u> day.
alliteration	Words starting with the <u>same sound</u>, e.g. <u>b</u>rilliant <u>b</u>rown <u>b</u>ear.
anecdote	A short, personal <u>story</u> that is usually <u>interesting</u> or <u>amusing</u>.
apostrophe	Used to show <u>possession</u>, e.g. "Ed<u>'s</u>", and <u>missing letters</u> in contractions.
assonance	Words that contain the <u>same vowel sound</u>, e.g. h<u>a</u>ppy bl<u>a</u>ck c<u>a</u>t.
audience	The person or people <u>reading</u> a text or <u>watching</u> a play.
autobiography	An <u>account</u> of someone's life story written by <u>that person</u>.
biography	An <u>account</u> of someone's life story written by <u>someone else</u>.
characterisation	The way a writer gives <u>information</u> about their <u>characters</u>.
clause	A part of a sentence which has a <u>subject and a verb</u>.
cliché	A <u>figure of speech</u> that has been <u>used a lot</u>.
colon	Used to introduce a <u>list</u> or an <u>explanation</u>.
comma	Separates items in a <u>list</u>, separates <u>extra information</u> and <u>joins clauses</u>.
contraction	The <u>new word</u> made by <u>joining</u> two words together with an <u>apostrophe</u>.
hyperbole	Deliberately <u>exaggerating</u> something to make an <u>unrealistic comparison</u>.
imagery	Descriptive language that <u>creates a picture</u> in the reader's mind.
irony	Saying <u>one thing</u> but <u>meaning the opposite</u>, e.g. "I'm so happy we lost."
metaphor	<u>Describing</u> something by saying that it <u>is</u> something else.
metre	The <u>rhythm</u> and <u>syllable pattern</u> of a poem.
mood	The <u>feel</u> or <u>atmosphere</u> of a text.
onomatopoeia	A word that <u>imitates</u> the <u>sound</u> it represents when you say it, e.g. "<u>buzz</u>".
paragraph	A <u>group of sentences</u> that talk about the <u>same thing</u>.
P.E.E.	<u>P</u>oint, <u>E</u>xample, <u>E</u>xplanation — a good way to answer reading questions.

personification	<u>Describing</u> something as if it were a <u>person</u>.
perspective	<u>Who</u> is telling a story.
phrase	A part of a sentence which <u>doesn't have</u> a <u>subject</u> and/or a <u>verb</u>.
plot	The events that <u>happen</u> in a story or play.
purpose	The <u>reason</u> for writing a text.
rhyming couplet	A <u>pair</u> of <u>rhyming lines</u> that are next to each other.
rhythm	A <u>pattern of sounds</u> created by arranging <u>stressed</u> and <u>unstressed syllables</u>.
semicolon	Used to separate <u>lists</u> of longer things and <u>join</u> sentences.
setting	<u>Where</u> a story or play takes place.
simile	<u>Describing</u> something by saying that it is <u>like</u> something else.
slang	<u>Informal language</u> which often sounds like natural <u>speech</u>.
speech marks	Used to show <u>direct speech</u>. They're also called <u>inverted commas</u>.
stage direction	An <u>instruction</u> in a play which tells an actor <u>how</u> to <u>speak</u>, <u>move</u> or <u>act</u>.
stanza	A <u>group of lines</u> in a poem, also known as a <u>verse</u>.
syllable	A <u>unit</u> of sound in a word, e.g. "jump" has one syllable, "jumping" has two.
symbolism	When something <u>stands</u> for something else, e.g. a lamb symbolises spring.
synonym	A word with the same or similar meaning to another word, e.g. <u>big</u> and <u>huge</u>.
theme	The <u>deeper meaning</u> of a story, e.g. love, power or greed, etc.

Index

EIRT1